Nurturing Different Dreams

Nurturing Different Dreams

Youth Ministry across Lines of Difference

Katherine Turpin

and

Anne Carter Walker

☙PICKWICK *Publications* · Eugene, Oregon

NURTURING DIFFERENT DREAMS
Youth Ministry across Lines of Difference

Pickwick Publications
An Imprint of Wipf and Stock Publishers
199 W. 8th Ave., Suite 3
Eugene, OR 97401

www.wipfandstock.com

ISBN 13: 978-1-62564-009-3

Cataloging-in-Publication Data:

Turpin, Katherine

Nurturing different dreams : youth ministry across lines of difference /
Katherine Turpin and Anne Carter Walker.

p. ; cm. —Includes bibliographical references.

isbn 13: 978-1-62564-009-3

1. Church work with youth. 2. Youth—Religious life. I. Walker, Anne Carter. II.
Title.

BV4447 N83 2014

Manufactured in the U.S.A.

Dedicated to the young women and men of FaithTrek
who shared their dreams with us

Contents

Acknowledgments

THIS BOOK WOULD NOT have come to be without the many participants, staff, and supporters of FaithTrek at the Iliff School of Theology. The complex and challenging environment enabled by the coming together of these many human lives birthed the reflections of this book. We are so grateful for the honor of having worked with all of you. In particular, we are grateful for Rebecca Youngblood, Donna Chrislip, and Angela Menke Ballou, who, along with Anne, wrote the initial grant proposal to the Lilly Endowment, Inc., that brought the program into being. Vincent Harding and Rachel Harding, and other staff members of the Veterans of Hope Project, were wise and consistent collaborators in making the program an intentionally diverse community that served young people well beyond the usual community of graduate theological education. Allyson Sawtell capably handled many logistical details as Associate Director in the early years and directed the program in its final year, and has been our cheerleader in the completion of this text. Andrew J. Ballou, Alicia Forde, EuKit Lim, Kristina Lizardy-Hajbi, and Yvonne Zimmerman provided reflections on their experiences and read drafts of early chapters and responded to them. In addition, Grant Gieseke, Katie Robb, and Sara Sutterfield Winn provided vignettes of their key experiences with the program. Although we were not able to include all of these stories in our final manuscript, they all informed our thinking. Our esteemed colleagues in the field of youth ministry, David F. White and Evelyn L. Parker, responded publically to early drafts of some of these chapters, and helped us to improve the manuscript with their insights and concerns. All of its shortcomings are, of course, our own.

Acknowledgments

In addition to funding the FaithTrek program through its years of existence, the Lilly Endowment, Inc., provided funding that allowed for research leaves and travel to allow for discussion and improvement of this text. We are grateful for their support in the creation of this text, and, especially, for nurturing both of our scholarly formations through their funding of the many programs exploring vocation and theological education with high school youth.

I, Katherine, am grateful for the love and support of my spouse, Andy Blackmun, who shows up for our family every day in countless ways to make life not only possible, but beautiful. Two of my three children came along in the years that I was involved in FaithTrek, and my hope for each of them is to find their way into multicultural communities in which to explore their own sense of vocation and the capacity to live into it.

I, Anne, wish to thank my parents, Jerald C. and Virginia Walker, and my sister, Lissa Walker, for your love, support, and good humor over these many years of my personal and professional growth. In addition, several mentors have been instrumental on my vocational journey. To Elizabeth Conde-Frazier, Andrew Dreitcer, Frank Rogers Jr., David F. White, and Rebecca Youngblood: thank you for calling out my God-given gifts when I could not see them, for challenging me beyond my felt capabilities, and for encouraging vocational directions that I myself could not imagine. A special thanks to my husband, Monty Gibson, for your constant challenge and care. May our young son, Ryan, also experience the invitation from God to explore his best gifts and the world's great needs in the midst of all of the incredible diversity that life has to offer.

CHAPTER 1

Difference and Dreaming

THE DREAMS OF YOUNG people matter. As Harlem Renaissance poet Langston Hughes envisions in his poem "Hold fast to dreams," dreams fuel life with energy and vitality, making possible creative choices and the agency to live into one's full capacity. [1] In another of his poems "Harlem," Hughes wondered about the destiny of a "dream deferred," wondering if it dried up like a raisin in the sun, stank like rotten meat, or exploded.[2] In these powerful images, Hughes explores both the essential power of dreams and the tragic costs of destroying them. As a person deeply immersed in the African American community in Harlem during the Great Depression, Hughes intimately understood the destruction of dreams by oppressive realities faced by people without access to the resources necessary to live into them.

As the prophet Joel claimed, and the writer of the book of Acts repeated, one sign of the presence of God's Spirit poured out on human flesh is a proliferation of dreams within God's people of all ages. To cultivate and honor dreams, to enliven the power of the imagination so that one can respond to God's call and live a worthy and faithful life is an essential task of youth ministry. In a culture of inequality of access to resources caused by historical legacies of racial and class privilege, this essential task can be hindered in significant ways. For many young people, particularly those

---

1 Hughes, *Selected Poems*, "Dream," 97.
2 Ibid., "Harlem," 61.

who come from nondominant or marginalized communities, dreams are at significant risk of being deferred, constrained, and denied.

Youth ministry that seeks to nurture the dreams of all young people takes up the challenge of both opening the capacity to dream and enlivening the agency to hold onto and live into those dreams. While the language of dreaming may evoke a sense of something ephemeral or fleeting, the work to help young people hold onto their dreams in the midst of conditions that deny, repress, or ridicule them requires tenacious and courageous intervention. Dreams are not expressions of wishful thinking, nor are they luxuries. They are an active expression of hope that allow young people to survive and thrive in the midst of the challenges of their daily lives. To attend to the dreams of young people in marginalized contexts requires much of the adults who hope to nurture them, particularly if those adults come from contexts where they have less experience of material poverty or less experience with racial or other forms of oppression. Nurturing different dreams requires increased intentionality and awareness.

Application Question: What dreams do you have of yourself at 35?

Participant Response: I hope I'm still alive when I'm 35.—Andre,[3] age 16

This application question to a summer youth ministry program and the honest response from a young African American participant documents a gap between the understanding of dreaming for the adult sponsors of the program and the reality of a life without dreams for a young male participant. While we have recorded a single response from a particular African American young man here, we received similar answers to this question from many of the fifteen to eighteen-year-old participants in the program. The questioning of survival well into adulthood did not come from over-dramatized youth speaking for effect. These were realistic assessments from youth who were intimately acquainted with the juvenile justice and foster care systems, who found school a place of struggle and alienation rather than a place of nurture and challenge, who had lived with violence at home or in their neighborhoods, and who had often already lost young friends and cousins to the harsh reality of their environment. They honestly did not know if they would still be around in twenty years, and

3. Names of all youth have been changed in order to provide confidentiality for youth participants.

they certainly were not given to dreaming about what their lives might be like in the future. The first occurrence of this response "If I'm still alive" was surprising to those of us who lead the program. The fourth or fifth instance called us to reconsider some of our basic assumptions about the practice of youth ministry in which we were engaged.

The question that we posed to Andre in the program's application indicates our belief that a primary goal of work with adolescents should be helping them to discern their vocation and to develop the agency and community support that enable living into it. What we quickly discovered was that our sense of this educational process was strongly identified with aspects of our race- and class-based privilege that the young people we worked with did not share, such as the practice of dreaming about one's future with some assurance that the future might occur. The experiences of coming to awareness of that privilege and how it shaped our practice of youth work are the seeds that grew into this book.

Often young people who do not share the same cultural background, material resources, and social entitlements evoke guilt-based inaction from persons with relatively greater privilege. To counter this inaction, this book advocates a risky, responsible engagement across lines of difference in youth ministry and other outreach projects with young people. Our belief is that, despite the many risks in working across boundaries of difference—particularly the risks of re-inscribing systems of domination and privilege while enacting race- and class-based injury—persons who hold relatively greater material and social resources have a responsibility to work across boundaries of difference in light of the potential for power-sharing and relational transformation possible through such encounters.

In this book we will describe, through stories and reflections from our own educational practice in a summer youth ministry and mentoring program called FaithTrek, the insights and challenges we faced in our particular context in building and enacting education with marginalized young people that is empowering, transformative, and liberating. We will offer concrete guidelines and practices that challenge those who work with youth in religious and secular settings not to succumb to guilt-based inaction, but rather to take up the practice of working with adolescents across lines of difference. In this sense, we recommend attending to the dreams of young people who come from different communities in an attempt to help them hold onto and live into their distinctive dreams.

While our experience emerged in a youth ministry setting, the concerns that we raise in this book are not exclusive to youth ministry. The tensions that we faced arise in any ministry or programmatic setting where well-intentioned persons with greater relative privilege and power are working with young people who hold less relative privilege or power. Such unequal relationships arise in public service settings where service providers hold greater material resources and access to institutional power than the populations they serve. They happen in teaching, where college-educated teachers work with adolescents who do not come from families with similar cultural capital. And they happen in religious education efforts, in camp and outreach settings where churches with material, social, and political resources want to work with "at-risk" youth or youth who simply don't come from the same social location as the sponsors and leaders of the event.

This book is not intended solely for educators and mentors who are white and middle class, though we think the insights of this book are deeply important for white, middle class readers because of the particular system of entitlement these combined social markers hold. We intend this text to address, more broadly, persons in educational and service settings where at least one element of their identity means that they have relatively greater power and privilege than those they serve or seek to serve. In this light, we understand identity markers such as race and class as cultural and political identities that are fluid and historical, changing from context-to-context. The fluidity of these cultural and political markers means that in one situation, one may have less relative privilege than others, while in another situation one may have greater power and privilege than those around them. This fluidity makes the educational encounter that much more complex, as no categorical schema is available to help persons identify times when they have greater relative privilege, and times when they have less privilege, complete with appropriate guidelines for engagement.

What we hope to offer here is our own reflection on the systems of entitlement and privilege that we embody as a result of our social location, detailing the ways these systems played out in our assumptions and practices in this particular instance of youth ministry. Our hope is that our reflections may encourage you to do similar reflection in your own work, and through this reflection begin to improve your capacity to help young people quite different from you to live into their dreams for their lives. In the next section, you will see us unpacking aspects of our own identities and how we understand these pieces of our identities to relate to systems of power and privilege. Our hope is that our narratives and the stories throughout this text will help you to explore your own identity in careful and nuanced ways in relation to the youth you hope to serve.

Who We Are

This book has two authors, though the insights in this book grow out of an experience of youth ministry that was collaborative and included many more people than just us. We'll start by giving you an idea of who we are, and along the way introduce our partners in this effort, as well as the context of the program from which the insights of this book emerged.

I, Anne, helped conceive of and directed FaithTrek, the context for youth ministry out of which the concerns for this book arise. A piece of my identity that is important to name is my racial/ethnic identity. I am both Anglo and Native American (Cherokee Nation). I am neither entirely Cherokee nor entirely Anglo. These two pieces of my background have made me keenly aware of my "white skin advantage"[4] yet at the same time, as a member of a tribe in which the group and its members are of primary importance, I hold a collectivist worldview that motivates me to work toward the liberation of the socially marginalized. My background originates in Oklahoma, where my parents were leaders in higher education. This means that I grew up in an elite educational setting, with constant exposure and access to people who were producers of knowledge. In addition, I attended only private schools throughout my education. Exposure to these educational settings provided me with a solid foundation for holding the resources necessary to access institutions of power with a sense of articulation and entitlement. For example, there was never a time that I imagined I would not go to college. The confidence that I would be admitted and eventually graduate from college was a given. I hold three advanced degrees, and therefore I have access to many resources and networks that can ensure my economic and professional stability and advancement.

I, Katherine, am academically trained as a theologian specializing in religious education, currently preparing clergy in graduate theological education. Because my family of origin was from the southern United States, "white" was the racial/ethnic identity category that was used to describe us rather than any historic sense of national heritage. As a heterosexual,

4. Case, "Claiming White Social Location," 71.

5

married parent of three children (elementary aged), my current family configuration places me in a dominant "normal" position in US culture. Several generations of my family were college educated prior to me. Like Anne, a professional and educated adulthood was expected for children in my family, placing us solidly in middle-class cultural norms. Because my grandparents served as clergy and teachers in rural areas of the Southern Appalachian region, "professional" and "impoverished" were not always mutually exclusive identity categories in our family experience. I was raised in suburban areas of major US cities (Houston, Birmingham), but my family culture retained its rural Southern roots in these places.

To go through this catalogue of identity categories can feel uncomfortable or even seem unnecessary, but being aware of social location and its attendant privileges and oppressions is an important practice in anti-oppressive multicultural religious educational settings. As you can tell from the above description, we both bear several identity markers of privilege in US culture: white, heterosexual, Christian, married, upper middle class, professional/graduate-educated, able-bodied, middle-adulthood, and of Anglo-descent. These identity markers mean that we have been raised to understand ourselves as "average Americans" though in fact we both inhabit a particular slice of that culture. The practice of naming these categories and being aware of the cultural values and biases inherent in them is critical to engaging in youth ministry across lines of race and class difference. Because the culture teaches dominant culture persons not to notice the specificity of our social locations, being aware of it requires intentionality. Youth ministry in particular teaches us to "look beyond" such identity markers toward spiritual elements of our being as if these embodied material elements of our being were divorced from our spiritual selves. Of late, some people dismiss this practice of attending to social location derisively as "political correctness." While it can be a disingenuous practice of lip service and uncommitted semantics, naming social location can also represent a much richer ethical commitment to noticing the structures of power that exist in our culture that we are taught to ignore, and therefore tend to impose on people without conscious reflection.

These contemporary identity categories emerge from long histories of social practice and relationship which we are carefully taught not to bring up in polite company. One strategy for changing the impact of these histories (which we do not advocate) is to ignore them. For example, many people rely on the concept of colorblindness, claiming not to "see" another's race, as a strategy for ignoring the complex and painful history of racing in this country. Unfortunately, while many claim that being colorblind helps them to see the "true person" behind the color of their skin, such a stance denies the shameful and violent history of racing in this country, and indeed causes one not to notice the complex histories and practices that shape identity. Such a stance denies both the particular ways that being raced contributes to the construction of identity at the same time that it ignores the important ethnically homogeneous cultures of solidarity and strength that have arisen in response to painful experiences of racialization.[5] We believe that such an approach denies the ongoing power and legacy of these histories, and the ways that we as persons of particular kinds of privilege both benefit from these histories and are complicit in their regeneration.

Risk and Responsibility

One of the hardest-won educational insights of the past century for persons identified with dominant culture is that we have tendencies towards domination and colonization at worst, and paternalism and charity at best when involved in educational efforts with people from nondominant social locations. From the history of missionary-run boarding schools and their terrorizing effects on American Indian peoples to more subtle practices of public education that replicate the ideals and values of certain dominant groups and denigrate the ideals and values of other groups through textbook illustrations and other forms of implicit curriculum, entering into education across boundaries of privilege risks the replication of systems of domination.[6]

However, there are real risks involved in choosing to work only with young people who share a social location of privilege as well. Working exclusively with those who are privileged denies the sharing of institutional resources (knowledge, materials, money) with folks who may not have as ready access to such resources. For instance, the Iliff School of Theology— the theological school that founded our program—is a predominantly white school with over a hundred years of accredited, degree-granting status and connections with the United Methodist Church, a powerful mainline denomination. Because of this, it had access to Lilly Endowment, Inc.,

5. Hearn, "Color-blind Racism," 272–88.

6. For more on colonizing aspects of education, see Lomawaima and McCarty, *To Remain an Indian*; Tinker, *Missionary Conquest*; Gonzalez et al., *Funds of Knowledge*.

who granted $1.2 million to the school to engage in theological exploration of vocation with high school aged youth. If the people given the power to administer that grant had decided to only recruit young people from communities that had a history with the school, we would have maintained those resources within the circles that had already benefitted from them and missed the opportunity and responsibility to literally share the wealth.

Opening one's self to risk, to the possibility of getting something wrong, is particularly counter-intuitive to the North American middle class, but exactly what we need to do to seek more liberating and transformative relationships and practices. Ethicist Sharon D. Welch describes this middle class avoidance of risk an "ethic of control," a need to "get it right" in our ethical endeavors. One manifestation of an ethic of control is "cultured despair," whereby middle class persons divest themselves of responsibility for those relationships, practices, and tasks that do not have measurable or resolvable outcomes, over which they cannot control.[7] A middle class ethic of control, says Welch, "assumes that it is possible to guarantee the efficacy of one's actions:"[8]

> The despair of the affluent . . . has a particular tone: it is a despair cushioned by privilege and grounded in privilege. It is easier to give up on long-term social change when one is comfortable in the present.[9]

Building upon Welch's analysis of middle class cultured despair, a common and often unconscious approach to youth ministry is to work only with those who are most like us, as doing so will cause the least relative discomfort to our sense of well-being. In this format for youth ministry, our primary ministry setting is with those from our own communities who look like us, behave like us, and carry common assumptions and values to ours. We still do "mission" work with the poor, but it is often in anti-relational settings, where we are not afforded opportunities to build relationships and seek mutual transformation with those whom we serve. Working across lines of difference where we are engaged in deeply relational work with people who are not like us means that we will not always know how to relate, how to make decisions, how to decide what is best. Such work causes discomfort and dissonance with one's general sensibilities and practices,

---

7. Welch, *A Feminist Ethic of Risk,* 40–41.

8. Ibid., 14.

9. Ibid., 41.

and therefore, we often avoid it. Furthermore, we are often taught in youth ministry settings to look past the particulars of individual differences toward the common bond of Christian fellowship. From this perspective, we are taught that any explicit recognition of human difference betrays the bond of fellowship of those baptized as followers of Jesus. As authors, we think this approach to youth ministry reinforces an ethic of control, and ultimately re-inscribes white and middle-class social domination.

A second problematic approach to youth ministry in light of Welch's ethic of control is to take steps toward working across lines of difference, but to do so in ways that maintain the overall comfort and inherent privilege and power of the middle class. In this model, we avoid practices that will display what we don't know, for once it is discovered that we do not have all of the answers, we lose a sense of competence. To be honest, even in settings in which persons of privilege are intentionally seeking to dismantle systems of power and oppression in working across boundaries of difference, the implicit maintenance of these oppressive social norms remains present. This is what makes youth ministry across lines of difference a particularly risky endeavor. Furthermore, engaging in risky behavior does not always sit well with standards of professional behavior that are a part of white, middle class cultural values. In such a cultural system, to be responsible means to be in control, to ensure correct outcomes, and at the very least to first do no harm.

Welch encourages those of us who are middle class and/or white to take up an "ethic of risk," making explicit recognition that our assumptions and practices are partial, and that we do not have all the answers. In this model, our knowledge of ourselves, of our neighbors, of the world around us expands as we "see the limits of our own vision"[10] and build solidarity and mutual transformation thorough "dialogue, mutual critique, and political action" with those who are not like us.[11] This text recognizes that risky behavior means that harm is going to be done. Harm in the form of race and class injury and the re-inscribing of systems of privilege is written in the histories of social identities that we embody and in the communities and values we inhabit. No magic antidote exists to counter this possibility. So the questions arise: What kind of risks are we willing to take to be in relationship, to try to be an adult mentor to a young person across boundaries of difference? What will we have to let go of? What will we have to learn?

10. Ibid., 139.
11. Ibid., 136.

Shared leadership in youth work across cultural groups is critical so that at least some of the adult leadership shares the same identity markers as young people from nondominant social groups. These leaders can better hear, recognize, and contribute to the emerging strength of the young people in ways that are authentic. Even better is for educational leadership and practices to emerge from nondominant communities themselves, addressing the cultural specificity of the challenges and strengths of those communities. Educators such as Ella Baker, Paulo Freire and Myles Horton have made powerful arguments for creating alternative, popular educational settings that skirt the systems created by dominant culture and emerge in dialogue with or wholly determined by marginalized communities.[12] Although we believe that marginalized communities benefit from self-determined, culturally specific educational settings, this book is not about creating such settings. Although we believe they are important, we also realize that the allocation of resources in our culture and the fact that many powerful institutions are dominated by people like us makes it important to address education across lines of difference. We think it is important to consider ethically what is best to do when dominant culture adults are engaging nondominant culture adolescents in an attempt to share institutional resources with those who do not already have easy access to those resources.

In our experiences of intercultural youth ministry, we have found ourselves occasionally failing miserably because of our own preconceptions, assumptions, habitual ways of teaching, and understandings that failed to connect with participants. To that extent, we are trying to share some of the ways we caught ourselves in these moments in the hopes that others will not repeat our mistakes. At the same time, we have had moments of transcendence, powerful transformational moments, where boundaries of difference and privilege seemed less tightly drawn, and where mutual learning occurred. This book isn't necessarily designed to provide inspirational accounts of these moments in the hopes that you will go and do likewise. This is a book that argues for self-conscious attention to the power dynamics and identity politics that are written into such occurrences so that practitioners can navigate a course in such situations that does not require them to deny their own privilege and power, their cultural background and

12. For examples of popular education and marginalized communities, see Freire and Horton, *We Make the Road*; Ransby, *Ella Baker*.

values, but also doesn't encourage them to impose them. It is about taking both the risk and the responsibility of engagement across lines of privilege.

Vignette—by Allyson Sawtell

It was day four of the first week of FaithTrek. We were still getting to know each other. We were exploring diversity—racial, physical ability, ethnic, theological, political—and learning about each other's lives. Four of the youth from Salt Lake City, who were Tongan, got word that a young cousin of theirs had died back home. They decided to remain at FaithTrek, and the community sought ways to care for them. One of those ways was in our communal worship experience, those diverse services from a variety of cultures and faith traditions that we held nearly every day throughout the program. That particular day, a FaithTrek staff person, Lili Stahlberg, was scheduled to lead a Romanian Orthodox service, to help the youth experience yet another way to worship and to pray. We talked to Lili about the situation, and she agreed to include an Orthodox memorial service as part of the larger service.

There we were in the chapel, African American, Spanish, Asian American, Latino/a, Korean, Northern Indian, Portuguese, Pacific Islander, and Anglo, ages fifteen through fifty. We were United Methodist, American Baptist, United Church of Christ, Episcopalian, Presbyterian, Buddhist, Mennonite, Lutheran, and Assembly of God. And worship began. Music, chanting, shared prayers, all amid the candles and incense and icons. In the liturgy of the Romanian Orthodox Church, we began to pray for peace for the young cousin, for his family and friends. We found ourselves all standing in the front of the chapel, holding beeswax tapers, and chanting, "May his memory be eternal." Tears were on the faces of the four Tongan youth, and on most of the rest of the faces as well. An adult-led Romanian Orthodox service ministered to the spirits of Tongan United Methodist youth. The power of the moment transcended culture and faith tradition, age and race and language and experience, and it settled in to surround us all. It was holy ground.

FaithTrek: Our Particular Journey

Our reflections about youth ministry across lines of difference arise from our experiences over five summers of living in residential community with older high school youth engaged in theological exploration of vocation. An intentionally ecumenical and culturally diverse community, FaithTrek was a grant-funded program designed to invite youth to live together with adults for three weeks at a graduate theological school, to reflect theologically on issues of identity, community, and vocation. We approached this youth ministry opportunity with the intent to broaden explorations of vocation with adolescents beyond the middle class, particularly to include those who did not have ready access to such resources for vocational exploration in their own communities. We also intended to compose a multicultural, multi-class learning community that would explore call and vocation together. While our reflections here are particularly focused upon working across boundaries of race- and class-based difference in this setting, we also worked with issues related to the nature of vocational explorations for youth from dominant backgrounds, with gay and lesbian youth, and with youth who experience significant physical and mental health challenges. These are all issues that deserve additional attention in published works by scholars of youth ministry. This book, then, explores one very prominent issue in the midst of many that were raised as we lived and worked together for three weeks every summer.[13]

The make-up of the FaithTrek youth population was significantly diverse, including youth from poor, working class, and middle class backgrounds. The youth who joined us came from numerous living situations: group foster homes, single parent families, two parent families, and collectives of parents, siblings, aunts, uncles and cousins. Some of the youth were able-bodied while at least one brought significant physical challenges, and many more brought learning and mental health challenges, and histories of physical, sexual, and emotional abuse. The youth were Tongan, African American, Chicana, Caucasian, Latino/a, South African, Romanian-American, Samoan, Korean-American, and much more. This group was also religiously diverse, representing a range of Christian and non-Christian religious commitments from Missionary Baptist, to Mennonite, to Buddhist, to Christian Orthodox. As we can see from Allyson's story about the power of this diversity in the midst of a community worship experience,

13. See Appendix 1 for an example of a typical day at FaithTrek.

this context could have transcendent experiences of connection. At other times, we struggled to connect with youth and honor their differences.

In reflecting upon experiential differences in the educational context, attention to the identities and perspectives brought by the adult educators at FaithTrek is critical. In light of our concern for the dynamics of teaching across lines of difference, the fact that the majority of the adult educators at FaithTrek were working on or held a graduate or undergraduate degree matters. While the leadership reflected cultural/ethnic diversity (African American, Romanian, Caucasian, Native American, Chicana, Chinese, Caribbean-American, Korean, Naga, and more), we all held significant cultural capital—resources such as higher education, capacity to navigate institutions, and social and professional networks that allow for participation in centers of power that make public expressions of agency possible. Although some of us started from poor or working class backgrounds, almost all of us held the markers of middle class existence as adults, and we all held a particular power in that community as the adults in control of shaping and enforcing the program's educational environment and pedagogy.[14]

Our particular commitment to youth ministry at FaithTrek—and our commitment to youth ministry that provides the foundation for this book—is that youth ministry involves developing the vocational identity of young people. Vocational identity forms through the exploration of adolescents as they find ways to partner with God in God's work in the world, confirming their identity and particular dreams in relation to God and the world.[15] Therefore, activities at FaithTrek focused on identifying and reflecting upon how one understands the self, identifying spaces and places where God is enlivening the spirit, as well as exploring the places where one's heart is breaking for the world. One of the practices we employed at FaithTrek to help the youth name and explore their own gifts and passions was "Appreciative Inquiry" (AI).[16] Originally an organizational development model that helps human systems to identify best practices, we employed AI to help the youth name and attend to those places in their own lives where their passions were ignited, where their gifts were used to their

14. This is not intended as a blanket statement, given our argument for the fluidity of identity. For example, some among us had greater privilege in addition to our education background, such as being white and heterosexual, while others among us represented target groups in addition to their educational resources, such as being non-Christian, LGBT, or not American citizens.

15. Fowler, *Becoming Adult, Becoming Christian*, 115.

16. Whitney et al., *The Power of Appreciative Inquiry*.

fullest, and were they felt they were making a real difference in the world.[17] In nightly "Covenant Groups," the youth would explore these issues with a consistent group of peers and adults who would guide them through the interviews and reflections on their gifts. This was often a place of validation and comfort, but also a space of encounter with difference where youth were exposed with interests and gifts that were significantly different from their own.

FaithTrek included social-critical dimensions as well, as one cannot simply affirm the positive but must also engage the places in the world that need healing, including a critical assessment of the social, cultural, and economic dimensions of life. The primary location for this activity was the program's "Discovery Groups," where youth would explore issues like gender and sexuality, race and class, environmental concerns, and interfaith engagement. Discovery groups happened not only in the classroom, but also in the community where they engaged with the issues they studied in the reality of the everyday. For example, the group studying the dynamics of race and class visited a local homeless ministry in downtown Denver; the politics and religion group visited the headquarters of Focus on the Family in nearby Colorado Springs. As an integrative component, youth were invited to express and to reflect upon the intersection of their emerging understandings of self and call with the needs of the world through artistic expression, reflective prayer and youth-created worship services. We hoped to construct a community in which the youth would develop a number of important capacities—personal reflection, negotiations in community, artistic expression, prayer and worship, critical study—to help them "listen for the voice of vocation."[18] In this sense, then, we sought to bring integration to Frederick Buechner's concept of vocation as "the place where your deep gladness and the world's deep hunger meet."[19] We explore these elements of youth ministry further in the final chapter, describing approaches and strategies to engage them with youth.

17. Here's a sample starter for an Appreciative Inquiry type interview: Tell me about a time when you felt really alive, like you were using your gifts and skills to the fullest, where you felt connected to your inner self, to those around you, and to the world—where you really felt at home in the universe. What was it about that experience that made you feel so alive and connected? What were you doing? Who was there? What were the people around you doing? What were the conditions that made this such a high point for you?

18. Palmer, *Let Your Life Speak*.

19. Buechner, *Wishful Thinking*, 95.

Most importantly, our commitment to vocational exploration in youth ministry, at FaithTrek and in other youth ministry settings, seeks the active, public agency of youth as they come into expression of their identities and commitments in the world. Vocational development in this sense is not an isolated exploration of the identity or a silent meditation on God's purpose for one's life. It is an engagement with the passions and interests of the self as one interacts with the social world, expressed as the human spirit is enlivened to partner with God in changing the world. Exploring this sense of calling involves cultivating young people's sense of agency, their sense of individual and communal identity, and their dreams of what the world is and can become.

Research Approach

Leveraging the experiences and memories of our own memories and experiences as teachers and observers in the context of this program, we also spent countless hours talking with youth participants, reflecting with adult staff and mentors, and poring over program evaluations in an attempt to craft a program that reached our aims for empowering the youth in our midst. However, since neither of us was in a sustained classroom setting at Faith-Trek, it became important to seek out the narratives of other community members as we approached the writing of this book. Therefore, throughout the book you will encounter stories of those who taught at FaithTrek as they describe the particular tensions that arose as they sought to teach about identity, youth agency, and faith in this multicultural community.

This "grounded theory" approach to religious education research builds theory from data that starts as lived experience.[20] This model of qualitative research draws theoretical insights from the descriptive and reflective experiences of members of a particular community. For us, this approach involves describing situations where tensions across race and class emerged by collecting data through conversations, narratives, and interviews. We have worked to identify major themes within these narratives, to begin to formulate theories that can help us to learn more about the tensions we encountered.

Throughout the research process, there is an additional stage of verification: verifying within our community that the memories we are drawing upon and the theories that are emerging reflect the experiences and

20. Strauss and Corbin, *Qualitative Research.*

perspectives of those from whom the data was gathered. Toward this effort, we compiled a group of readers and conversation partners (both former adult staff members and former youth participants) who were members of the FaithTrek community, who could name aspects of FaithTrek that we did not see, respond to our initial thoughts and inclinations, and challenge us to think beyond the confines of our own experiences. An explicit limitation of our research is that the majority of the youth participants are not active participants in the current development of this book. This means that, while we seek to write about theories that accurately reflect the realities of the FaithTrek program, our insights are only partial in that they reflect the particular insights and tensions of those doing the *teaching* across boundaries of difference. We recognize this as a "colonizing aspect" of our research that we are writing "about subjects who are not empowered to talk back."[21]

We are both trained in the field of practical theology—a scholarly discipline in which theological reflections arise out of process of observing and interpreting the practices of communities of faith—and therefore we see this work as providing the foundation for subsequent practical theological reflections. The method of grounded theory is a helpful compliment to practical theology as it provides us tools for the critical exploration of our educational practices. Further development of this material toward a practical theological work could include reflection on what vocation looks like, theologically, from the perspectives of nondominant people.

An Invitation to Conversion

In the United States adolescents and young adults are becoming increasingly racially and socioeconomically diverse while the teaching population remains predominantly white and middle class. Many youth ministry programs that utilize volunteer mentors recruit adults who are ill-equipped to bridge cultural difference and effectively build sustainable relationships with adolescents who come from different backgrounds than their own. College and university campus ministries that are historically white struggle to provide adequate support and mentoring for students who traditionally have not been represented in the college population. Often, mentoring relationships break down over cultural misunderstandings because of misrecognition of the unspoken expectations valued by mentors and rejected by the young people. We believe that this book will assist such persons in

21. Bettie, *Women without Class*, 27.

analyzing and transforming their own practices of mentoring and teaching young people who come from different communities than their own.

A privileged position can make it difficult to hear and recognize the particular realities, dreams, and needs of adolescents from nondominant contexts. One ethical response might be to stop engaging in such ministry, to work primarily with those who are like us (who also require spiritual care and need to explore what vocation looks like in the context of an ethic of risk), and to become allies to persons from nondominant communities who wish to develop their own youth ministry. Regardless of what else we do, we should be working on issues of privilege and vocation in our own communities, striving to act as allies with nondominant groups where invited and to share what resources we can even as we ourselves are transformed by encounters with difference.

An additional practice—the one we advocate for and demonstrate in the writing of this book—is to consider doing the work of border-crossing youth ministry despite its risks. It is work that takes a revolution of the heart, a willingness to change deeply, and to give up power. Paulo Freire describes this boundary-crossing work a type of conversion: "Conversion to the people requires a profound rebirth. Those who undergo it must take on a new form of existence; they can no longer remain as they were."[22] The work of writing this text is a part of that conversion process, noticing wrongdoing and engaging in repentant changes of behavior. We also argue that a practice of conversion involves attending to the dynamics of power and privilege when working across boundaries of difference. This conversion will help practitioners engage in ministry that enhances the agency of young people to live into their own dreams.

There are no guarantees that we will get it right. Intercultural settings inevitably involve daily conflicts, embarrassing admissions, and occasional deep injuries. But doing this work anyway, despite the inherent risks, means that we can potentially get it less wrong as we practice border crossing youth ministry time and again. As a means of embracing risk, sharing power, enlivening youth agency, and transforming our understandings of self and other, we advocate engaging the work despite these risks.

22. Freire, *Pedagogy of the Oppressed*, 42–43.

CHAPTER 2

Power and Privilege

CONVERSATIONS ABOUT ISSUES LIKE power and privilege can make people feel uncomfortable in educational settings—particularly religious ones. We sometimes assume that in a religious environment power and privilege should not be noticed or discussed. Hierarchies of power might be minimized because of a shared commitment to equality in the eyes of God. As the Christian sacred text proclaims: "There is no longer Jew or Greek, there is no longer slave or free, there is no longer male and female; for all of you are one in Christ Jesus" (Galatians 3:28). Sometimes participants equate noticing and naming differences in power as an act of perpetuating those differences rather than working for their transformation. Many a time, youth have said their leaders: "We were getting along fine until *you* brought this race thing up. This is *your* problem, not ours." Because of the ways these power structures often go unnoticed to us as a norm, as "just the way things are," we think that naming and addressing these issues are a core feature of any youth ministry that involves intercultural work.

We believe that you can't address power disparities and the social structures that cultivate privilege and oppression without talking about these issues. We also think that we, as Christians, are called to such work. It is part of our human vocation to address the inequities and disparities that keep us from fully loving our neighbors and participating with God in the cultivation of more just communities with shared access to the goodness that life affords.

In order to talk about issues of privilege and oppression, and how these concepts connect to our relationship with youth and to our broader ministries, we need to be clear about what we mean by the various terms we are using. So, even though you may find it uncomfortable to read through some of this, and you may find it even more uncomfortable to talk about these issues in your own ministry, we think the stumbling blocks you might encounter if these topics remain below the surface far outweigh the discomfort of the conversation.

Defining Terms

When we began our work at FaithTrek, we carried a commitment to multicultural religious education. We thought it was important to bring a diverse group of adults and youth together, in the hopes that doing theological reflection in a diverse community would help us all to reflect more fully on the role that social location plays in the development of vocational identity. We still think that a multicultural context is important for good critical thought and vocational development to happen, but we think it is important to be clear what we mean by "multicultural religious education."

Multicultural religious education must do more than simply celebrate the rich cultures among us and the ways that this diversity reflects God's creative design. Multicultural religious education must include an anti-oppressive focus. This means that our education needs to pay attention the ways that social structures pave the way for the vocational dreams of some and obstruct the dreams of others. *Anti-oppressive religious education* focuses directly on the cultivation of critical thinking so that we might understand why and how society maintains privilege and oppression, and, for youth ministry, how this contributes to the ways youth understand themselves, their vocational possibilities, and their understanding of God's call for their lives.

For this reason, we have decided to use terms like "privilege" and "oppression" more often than "multicultural" or "cross-cultural" in order to recognize that different social locations and cultural groups have different institutional power in North American culture. Particularly when we are working in ministry settings from a position of institutionalized power—where we hold more social privilege as those we minister with—we believe there is an ethical imperative to take that power and privilege seriously rather than to follow the cultural norms to downplay or deny that power.

So, what do we mean by privilege, and what kind of power do privileged people hold? When we are talking about people holding particular *social privilege*, we are saying that persons in certain social groups—men, white people, the middle and upper economic classes, heterosexuals, the able-bodied, US citizens, and Christians, among others—possess the unearned ability to express forms of domination and social entitlements because we belong to these social groups. By simply belonging to a variety of social groups, some of us are afforded advantages. We did not earn these advantages, nor are they obvious to those who receive them.[1]

Sometimes designations such as race or social class are thought of as biological or part of the natural order of things. However, these race and class demarcations have been constructed by society in order to shape our common life with distinctions of difference used to reward a minority with elite status and to marginalize and disenfranchise a majority as socially deviant.[2] For example, while no scientific evidence exists to delineate biological differences between people based upon skin color, over time societies have created categorical divisions called "race" and attached characteristics of attribution and behavior to those groups based upon skin color, shape of body and face, and texture of hair. The privileges that we attach to race, social class, gender, and other categories of privilege are not the result of biological fact or the natural order of things. Rather, these privileges are the result of a process of objectification and internalization whereby we associate some groups as morally and socially superior and other groups as morally and socially deviant. Thus, though I (Anne) was born with white skin, it is the way society objectifies white skin and provides me rewards based upon my skin color that gives me advantage. I did not earn these advantages; they simply exist because my white skin has become associated as a positive attribute by dominant culture, and I am rewarded for that through the subtleties of daily social interaction as well as through the accrued material benefits of long histories of institutional and systemic discrimination.

Theorist Peggy McIntosh teaches us that the advantages associated with privilege take two forms: *unearned entitlements* and *conferred dominance*. The first of these, unearned entitlements, she describes as rights that should not have to be earned, but that society sets aside as entitlements afforded to a select few. For instance, McIntosh notes that the basic human

1. McIntosh, "White Privilege," 82.
2. Hobgood, *Dismantling Privilege*, 12.

need for belonging is an entitlement that all persons should be afforded.[3] This belonging provides us access to the communities, services, and institutions that are necessary to be clothed and fed, to find affordable housing and medical care, to build community and create a common life. Though entitlements such as belonging should exist for all, McIntosh notes, "At present, since only a few have it, it is an unearned advantage."[4]

An equally insidious advantage we receive when we belong to privileged groups is access to conferred dominance. Conferred dominance, says McIntosh, "Gives permission to control, because of one's race or sex [or religion, or sexual orientation]."[5] Conferred dominance is present, for example, by the very fact that we as people with various privileges can choose when and how to engage issues of privilege and oppression, or simply to ignore them. It is this agency—the unearned ability to choose our comforts and discomforts—which our privilege affords us.[6]

But dominance goes far beyond the choices we make to engage issues of injustice. Because people with privilege are the primary historical and cultural shapers of the society we all live in, people in dominant groups decide what counts as legitimate knowledge and who makes crucial decisions, which voices are heard and which are silenced, who receives resources and who does not. Further, because people with privilege are the primary shapers of our collective life, the social and cultural practices cultivated by those in power appear as the "norm" by which we all live. So, while dominance doesn't look like one person putting a "boot to the neck" of another person (so to speak), it is the cumulative historical effect of less dramatic social practices that legitimize and resource some, to the neglect of others, that composes social privilege, and the unfortunate result is a system of inequalities that appears "normal."

There are those, however, who can easily detect that this norm is not right. Those who are the recipients of domination—women, people of color, non-Christians, non-citizens, homosexual, bisexual, and transgendered persons, and those who are disabled, among others—consistently encounter and are confronted by our expressions of entitlement and domination. Audre Lorde calls this endorsement of all things privileged as the center of reality the "mythical norm:"

3. McIntosh, "White Privilege," 84.
4. Ibid.
5. Ibid., 83.
6. Wildman, *Privilege Revealed*, 16.

> Somewhere, on the edge of consciousness, there is what I call a mythical norm, which each one of us within our hearts knows "that is not me." In America, this norm is usually defined as white, thin, male, heterosexual, Christian, and financially secure. It is with this mythical norm that the trappings of power reside within this society. [7]

Through this imaginary norm, dominance comes to appear as the natural order of things—the way life should be. However, those who experience the expressions of entitlement and the domination of the privileged know very well that this is not and should not be the norm. These persons, whom we will refer to as *nondominant* or *oppressed*, often do not have ready access to the basic social entitlements needed to access networks and obtain resources for the well-being of themselves and their families. As Allan Johnson states, "Just as privilege tends to open doors of opportunity, oppression tends to slam them shut."[8] These dynamics of entitlement, advantage, and domination often play out in subtle day-to-day interactions that are easily ignored by persons who benefit from them, and may not experience themselves as privileged or advantaged in any way.

You may be thinking to yourself: I am a white, heterosexual woman, which means that my social location is dominant in the categories of race (white) and sexual orientation (heterosexual), but nondominant in the category of gender (woman). I don't always *feel* oppressed. At the same time, I know what it is like to be a woman in a man's world (*sic*). How can I be both privileged and oppressed, dominant and nondominant, at the same time? Many, if not most, of us experience both privilege and oppression, because of the varieties of roles and identities that make up our social locations. There are very few people who experience "pure" privilege or "pure" oppression. Instead of seeing privilege as "one, overarching structure," theorist Patricia Hill Collins helps us to view this dynamic as an interlocking "matrix of domination."[9] Collins writes, "A matrix of domination contains few pure victims or oppressors. Each person derives varying amounts of penalty and privilege from multiple systems of oppression which frame everyone's lives."[10] By thinking of privilege and oppression operating as a matrix, and not as a fixed structure, we can think of our own identities

---

7. Lorde, *Sister Outsider*, 116.

8. Johnson, *Privilege, Power, and Difference*, 38.

9. Collins, *Black Feminist Thought*, 222.

10. Ibid., 229.

as fluid. Depending upon the circumstances of our social encounters, we sometimes are recipients of privilege and we sometimes experience the pressures of oppression—and sometimes we experience these both at the same time, whether we know it or not. Written language fails to capture the complexity and fluidity of social location within the matrix of domination, so we use "dominant" as shorthand name throughout this text for persons who benefit from privilege in a given context because of some element of their complex social location. We hope when you hear that term you can call to mind the intricacy of the social reality it is meant to convey.

The Value of Multicultural Religious Education

Despite the dynamics of power and privilege operating in multicultural settings, we are still advocating for diverse contexts of religious education. Engagement across racial, economic, and even religious lines provides an important context for the clarification of values, identity, and commitments that we think is a part of vocational identity formation. We often assume that young people need a consistent atmosphere for values clarification in order to form their sense of identity, which should include exposure to one set of values and norms. While the rich and consistent exposure to a particular tradition is helpful in initial formation, by older adolescence, this opportunity to live in diverse community can be deeply important to the formation of identity and vocational understanding in broader social contexts.

By encountering persons who come from different communities, often with different styles of being, youth come to see their own commitments and values in a new way. By virtue of contrast with other participants, they are able to see who they have been formed to be and to begin to discern what might be the limitations and gifts of the perspective of their community of origin. This interaction allows them to broaden their sense of their gifts, sometimes naming gifts that emerge from their background that have been latent because they seem "normal" in that environment. In the encounter with other's visions and norms, their own perspective is more clearly defined and at times called into question. This experience is a critical step in the claiming of identity and vocation.

Experiences with difference point toward the fact that vocational exploration for youth cannot be conceived simply as a passive task of identity development. Educational theorist Henry Giroux expands our vision of education for vocation with his insistence that education be viewed as a democratic process. Democracy, for Giroux, involves access to the resources and systems necessary to be self-determining, and to possess the resources necessary to contribute to the creation of public life (knowledge, values, and systems). Giroux advocates educating students toward their rights and responsibilities as citizens, helping them understand issues of inclusion and exclusion, of domination and subordination, and providing opportunities for public engagement.[11]

With this view of democratic education in mind, then, we come to understand the multicultural context of religious education not only as a process of identity development, but also as a political process empowering the social agency of youth as citizens of the world through critical thinking and social action. In this context, we must consider carefully who has power and who does not and how that agency (or lack thereof) has been shaped by social forces. We then enact religious education that takes seriously the creation of vocational identities amidst experiences of both entitlement to vocation and public participation and alienation from it. These kinds of identity politics are essential to understanding how one is in relationship to the structures and histories that one lives within and to discerning who one is called to be in the midst of them.

One of the ways that we found value in the multicultural context for youth without ready access to cultural and social capital was exposure to adults from a similar cultural group who modeled constructive encounters across lines of race and class. We remember one such encounter, when Daryl, an African American male, seized an informal opportunity to educate African American youth how to engage with dominant culture people—namely, white youth and adults. In taking up the task of showing these youth how to engage across lines of race and class with dominant-group people, Daryl was sharing important social and cultural capital with these youth—he was sharing the skills of how to negotiate relationship in a multicultural world.

Facing the Emotions Of Learning in a Multicultural Context

When recognition of the matrix of domination is present, some youth can readily craft confident vocational visions while others have not been taught

11. Giroux, *Living Dangerously*.

to interpret themselves as competent individuals, let alone empowered so-cial agents. Either way, the sense of self is distorted. Privileged students, while able to readily reflect upon their families of origin and imagine mul-tiple sites for finding a home, are largely unaware of the ways in which they are socialized into a culture of entitlement at the expense of others. Students from socially and economically marginalized backgrounds often have more fragmented geographical and family histories, experiencing vio-lence, neglect and psychological abuses. In light of such realities, it can be difficult for some marginalized youth to imagine a life direction beyond their immediate circumstances, and any sense of social agency or broader ability for cultivating the vocational imagination is seemingly out of reach.

Religious education for more privileged students does not only involve clarifying identity in relation to the family of origin and in light of one's gifts and passions. It also includes a critical engagement with the realities of systems of entitlement, connecting the construction of vocational identity to the dismantling of cycles of domination. By contrast, vocational educa-tion for youth from marginalized backgrounds requires a mining of the resources they currently hold as forms of resistance, subversion, creativity, and sustenance that can be mobilized toward the crafting of their voca-tional dreams. And, because we all operate in a significantly fluid matrix of domination, most good religious education for vocational development also includes attention to the building of critical awareness and the ability to read the patterns of inclusion/exclusion around us.

Shame, Guilt, and Anger

In a multicultural context, embarrassment, shame, guilt and anger often come up as youth and mentors within the privilege/oppression matrix face the realities of social inequality. Cognitive discomfort is a natural part of the learning process, and, when encountering revelations of social inequal-ity, emotional stress soon follows. As Beverly Daniel Tatum describes in relation to white racial identity development, white people encountering revelations of systemic inequality and racial prejudice can experience a sense of cognitive dissonance, because their encounters with structural in-equality challenge the myth of individual merit that has constructed their self-understandings.[12] Understanding systems of inequality challenges privileged people's core thinking about how the world works, which can be

12. Tatum, *"Why Are All the Black Kids,"* 98.

very disruptive and uncomfortable. Jean Piaget describes this dissonance in the process of learning as a loss of cognitive equilibrium. Piaget wrote that when new information is received via a person's encounter with a particular environment or source, the person seeks to incorporate the experience/information into her existing cognitive schemes (e.g., what she already knows). This organization of and adaptation to new information or new experience causes a lack of cognitive balance, during which the person must either "assimilate" the new information into existing cognitive schemes, or "accommodate" her cognitive schemes to meet the challenges of the new information, thus reaching a new state of equilibrium.[13]

For people with privilege, the tasks of encountering new information about systemic oppression, thinking critically about these realities, and seeking to understand these dynamics deeply can cause confusion, disbelief, and denial. In this sense, the dynamics of privilege and oppression can be hard to learn. Cognitive dissonance can cause grief and anger, as one tries to reconcile new information with what one previously knew to be true about one's self, about one's family of origin, and about how the world works.

When these feelings of cognitive dissonance arise for privileged people, often feelings of guilt and shame follow. Frances E. Kendall notes that when we are exposed to the pain associated with experiences of oppression, guilt often emerges as a sense of not knowing how to respond to or repair instances of injustice, or of responding out of a sense of obligation to do something about the problem.[14] Regardless of whether guilt results in inaction or in misguided action, it is a complex emotion that has self-serving ends, that is, the cessation of the discomfort felt when one encounters revelations of the pain associated with the dynamics of privilege and oppression. Though not terribly productive players in multicultural learning contexts, shame and guilt will arise, and religious educators can anticipate and address these emotions as they become present.

For nondominant persons, revelations of social inequality bring up another set of equally challenging emotions. Unlike their privileged counterparts, nondominant people (youth and adults) are quite aware of the realities of social inequality, having lived with the pressure of oppression for their entire lives. The realities of privilege and oppression are not always revelations, as they often are when encountered by privileged people.

13. Piaget and Inhelder, *Psychology of the Child*, 6.
14. Kendall, *Understanding White Privilege*, 103.

However, complex emotions can arise when nondominant people are in deep encounters with privileged people, especially when engaging issues of race, culture, and inequality. The emotions that might arise can be multiplied when those from nondominant social categories encounter people with privilege who are themselves encountering revelations of systemic injustice. Anger and frustration are likely to emerge when a nondominant person observes a dominant-culture person grappling with social inequality. Embarrassment and deep sadness can also emerge, as memories of trauma may arise when the pain and pressure of oppression are addressed publically. Tatum teaches us that, for nondominant adolescents working on the project of racial identity development, the "encounter" stage of development is often precipitated by an encounter with white culture, during which the nondominant youth is forced "to acknowledge the personal impact of racism."[15] When this occurs, nondominant youth often develop coping strategies which look like defiance or denial. Tatum calls this the development of an "oppositional social identity," whereby one keeps a distance from the dominant group, protecting one's emotional and even physical well-being.[16] While people in dominant groups often want to "talk it out" and engage at this point, nondominant group members may wisely retreat as an effort toward self-protection.

This dynamic often emerged during our work with multicultural learning communities. For example, in the first days of our time together one summer, members of the staff were concerned that a group of youth from a nondominant social category were dining together and not mingling with other youth at mealtimes. The concern was that these youth were not taking full advantage of the multicultural context, and would not be exposed to the benefits of multicultural community. One of the African American staff members reminded us that these youth were steeped in multicultural community—sharing rooms with kids from different communities, in classes with even different groups, and riding on the bus to various activities with a large population of youth who were different than them. In an environment where youth were experiencing this much diversity for the first time in their lives, mealtime was a touch point; a place to take a break, breathe, laugh, and find solidarity with their same-culture cousins and friends. Attending to the need for moments of connection within one's own group in

---

15. Tatum, "*Why Are All the Black Kids*," 55.
16. Ibid., 60.

the midst of multicultural encounter became an important act of solidarity between staff members and youth from nondominant groups.

In contexts of multicultural religious education with an anti-oppressive focus, feelings of guilt, shame, anger, and embarrassment are likely to arise for both adults and youth. The more productively we can anticipate and openly address these issues, the more fully we can live into a vision of the peaceable realm. Though we cannot promise to "fix" these challenging emotions, later in this chapter we will offer some resources that we think can help communities of multicultural learning work through them.

Dominant-Class Desire to "Get It Right"

First, we need to address a common desire that arises for dominant-class persons in settings of multicultural learning: the middle-class need to "get it right" that we spoke about in the first chapter. "Getting it right" often means relating, communicating, and negotiating in ways that are relevant and keep the peace with those in nondominant groups. As mentors, we often want to be above reproach in our work. At its best, this desire appropriately recognizes the potential for re-injuring persons in racist and classist ways that we want to avoid.[17] At its worst, it reflects the shame and guilt that rise up as we seek to assimilate the realities of domination as a social, cultural, and personal reality.

We want to be professional, in control, multiculturally aware, and appropriate. We want to appear to be managing conflict well. At times, this desire to get it right leads to defensiveness rather than responsiveness when we discover the ways in which our educational leadership has missed the mark. This desire proves particularly unhelpful when we come up against irreducible conflicts in a situation because of the history of racial and class relationships in broader culture, particularly when our own social location in terms of race and class identity becomes a barrier before we say or do

---

17. Talvacchia (*Critical Minds*, 22) notes, "We are confronted with a situation of our own ignorance about an issue, which, when revealed, can create tremendous divisiveness and personal hurt for the person in the targeted group. To make a mistake through our unintentional ignorance is not just to misunderstand, but to unwittingly cause hurt, and this foments a deeper resentment from the person who is a member of the targeted group. The unfortunate logic of oppression revolves around the fact that members of the dominant culture often cannot see the ways in which they discriminate. There is a great deal at stake in the mistakes we make as teachers and learners in multicultural settings."

anything as a leader. This defensiveness can be more about our desire to be above reproach than our desire to be an effective leader in this setting.

As dominant culture leaders, we cannot always trust our instincts in multicultural settings. One of the hallmarks of reflective teaching practice is that eventually it moves from conscious to unconscious behavior. However, many instincts honed in more predominantly white settings do not serve us well in multicultural settings. For example, Kathleen Talvacchia notes that the hallmark of good multicultural education is the presence of constructive conflict in the classroom: "In fact, if we are teaching in a diverse setting and inter-group conflict is not being worked through on some level, then we can be certain that we are not engaging the diversity properly or teaching effectively."[18] In other words, the lack of conflict probably indicates that white cultural norms are overriding other voices in the room. As white people, we have to learn that conflict—even at times heated conflict—may be a sign that good education is happening (remember, dissonance and learning go hand-in-hand). This is counterintuitive to many of the cultural norms of professional behavior in white North American culture, where conflict indicates a lack of control of the situation.

While letting go of the need to "get it right" does not give us a free pass to slack off on striving for excellent teaching, it does remind dominant-class people that humility is an important virtue for as we venture into multicultural educational settings as a leader. Relying on our intuitive sense of what will work often leads to a path that reinforces racial and class hierarchy in ways we may not even be aware. A willingness to work in the midst of uncertainty rather than out of an easy, "expert" authority can allow for authentic forms of multicultural interaction to occur. In this matrix of domination, with its dissonance-inducing encounters in which emotions are likely to become intense, where some will fight and some will flee, conflict is inevitable. How we enter and engage that conflict determines whether good multicultural religious education is possible.

18. Ibid.

Vignette—by Anne Carter Walker

It was our final "Town Hall" meeting at FaithTrek. Town Hall was the place where we would make decisions about our common life and address community conflicts. At this particular meeting, we were deciding how we would spend our final days together, what our final worship would look like, and who would be responsible for decorating for our farewell banquet. At the end of this meeting, Emmett, who had a knack for "rallying the troops" said, "You know, we've really gotten close during these meetings—closer than anywhere else." Then he turned to me, the camp director, and said, "We don't have to do this anymore, do we?"

Conflict as a Marker of Good Multicultural Religious Education

Adjudicating conflict is an important feature of any multicultural community. With recognition of the race- and class-based hierarchies that are present within such communities and the histories of power that accompany of these hierarchies—as well as the many cultural and relational challenges that we have already named as bringing challenges to border crossing religious education—conflict is an inevitable aspect of life together. In the midst of border-crossing encounters, we will disagree, misunderstand, and intentionally or unintentionally cause pain and injury to one another. As Emmett shows us in the side bar, addressing conflict can bring us more fully together, but it is not a space free of discomfort and pain that youth enter gladly.

Given constructive tools for covenant-making and for working through disagreements and injuries in ways that share power, we believe that addressing conflict can be one of the most transformative spaces in multicultural youth ministry. Furthermore, in a world in which youth have very few spaces to be a part of processes of decision-making related to how they will behave and move in the world, how they will relate to others, and how they themselves want to be treated, addressing conflict in youth ministry can provide a space for youth to experience and express agency. In working through conflict, youth become active participants in deciding what common life together will look like and how to keep one another—and the adults—accountable to those decisions. Unfortunately, we do not always respond to conflict in ways that share power and enliven youth agency. Before looking at some helpful practices for addressing conflict in multicultural communities with youth, we want to look more closely at some common responses to conflict.

Common Approaches to Conflict

There are two common approaches to conflict that we have found to inhibit youth agency and to maintain the dominance of adult leaders. The first approach, which we believe adolescents are most accustomed to, is a punitive approach. If adolescents wrong one another, the adults often decide on the most appropriate form of punishment and "hand down" that punishment to the youth, who either accept the punishment passively or "act out" by expressing resistance to the punishment. This approach to conflict with youth does not treat them as agents with the ability to determine the content of their lives and relationships, and therefore communicates that young people cannot be trusted to maintain healthy relationships. Unfortunately, youth are socialized in many educational settings to anticipate this response by adults. Often, in situations of conflict and disagreement at FaithTrek, when enacting models of community discernment to address issues of conflict or wrongdoing, the youth would say, "Could you just punish us?" reflecting how deeply disempowered these young people felt in relation to issues of conflict in their own lives. This is an approach to handling conflict that we believe is developmentally inappropriate for youth, who build strong skills for critical thinking and self-reflection in the adolescent years.

The second common approach to addressing conflict is to do nothing about it, to "brush it under the rug," or to deal with the conflict very privately so as not to "air our dirty laundry." This response to conflict likewise gives no indication to youth that they are responsible agents with a measure of control over the realities of their lives and the relational experience of the communities in which they participate. Further, this approach reflects a culturally white response to issues of disagreement or injury. With recognition of the ways in which whites express a need to maintain control of circumstances and surroundings, there is often the mentality among white leaders that conflict reflects a failure of leadership; the inability of adult leaders to maintain control and harmony in the group. Furthermore, for the sake of comfort, the maintenance of control, and the expression of cultural norms of "getting along" dominant people in multicultural spaces often avoid bringing up issues of divergence, disagreement, or conflict. In this dynamic, the privileged among us maintain our comfort and claim little responsibility for the relational issues that arise. This response to conflict leads the persons in our midst who represent target groups to shoulder the responsibility of initiating points of conflict. In this sort of multicultural setting where the leaders are predominantly white and conflict is instigated by people of color, bringing up conflict is often viewed by white leaders as an insult to the well-meaning efforts to create spaces of multicultural mutuality. This dynamic dismisses those who initiate conflict as troublemakers, or the "squeaky wheel."

As leaders, our impulse is often to come to quick resolution of an issue so that we can reflect the multicultural harmony toward which we aspire. However, we want to suggest that creating deep relationships across lines of race and class cannot be achieved without the hard work of engaging conflicts directly and in a sustained way.

Conflict as Encounter

The first step in this process, for leaders with social privilege, is to transform our understanding of conflict from something unhealthy and shameful toward an understanding of conflict as a natural and healthy aspect of life together. The concept of "encounter" can help us think differently about conflict in multicultural community. Encounter describes those spaces where cultures meet, where difference is experienced, and where values converge. Encounter necessarily involves interactions with different ways of doing and being, knowledge and values that are outside of the norm. As Ting-Toomey and Oetzel teach us, it is the encounter with differing cultural values, "a set of priorities that guide desirable or undesirable behaviors or fair or unfair actions," that often leads to conflict.[19]

Because multicultural encounter means engaging at the value-level, and given how deeply-felt value norms are to cultures and individuals, discomfort will be a necessary part of the interaction. Elizabeth Conde-Frazier writes:

> An encounter is where we risk. It is a place for the collision of
> two worlds—for the multiplicity of views. It is where various

19. Ting-Toomey and Oetzel, *Managing Intercultural Conflict*, 10.

> streams meet. It is the bringing together of a variety of sources
> that might not often be placed together. This is the borderland . . .
> It is straddling cultures. It is hearing multiple voices, at times with
> conflicting messages.[20]

Conde-Frazier wisely describes the space of encounter as one of risk. The reality is that those who have been historically marginalized enter encounter with full recognition of that risk. For persons who have experienced marginalization, entering into relationship with members of the dominant culture includes knowingly opening oneself to the possibility of injury.

We who are dominant often do not fully appreciate the great risks that are taken by those who are marginalized in entering spaces of multicultural encounter. We also fail to acknowledge that entering such spaces involves the taking of intentional risks for us, too. The risks we must take, however, look entirely different than the risks taken by persons who have been targeted as recipients of injustice. Risk for dominant group people is about surrender and sharing power. It includes the risk of wrestling with feelings of shame, guilt, and incompetence. The risk is knowing we will not always be in control, and we will not find easy answers and quick resolutions to the struggles that arise.

For those of us with more social power, we must recognize that part of the encounter will likely include significant anger and rage directed toward us from those in our community who experience domination. This anger is a mechanism of self-protection, a means for targeted persons to express resistance to domination. Conde-Frazier writes, "Beyond survival, anger also serves social transformation. We must combine our anger with the spiritual discipline of temperance so that it can be cooled to a productive level and can bear the spiritual fruits of justice, love, hope and peace."[21] As people with privilege, part of the work of facing this anger directed toward us is to understand that this anger is part of what has helped marginalized people survive. We need to stay in the moment of encounter and to strive to understand the source of the anger in order to make possible a transformative space for understanding and healing.

Encounter is about the meeting of two—or more—cultures in the generation of new ways of being in relationship, of new knowledge. Grappling with privilege and oppression, and seeking new ways of being in

20. Conde-Frazer et al., *A Many Colored Kingdom*, 176.
21. Ibid., 193–94.

multicultural relationship, takes emotional maturity and persistence. It requires a commitment to sustained relationships, where working through conflict becomes a process of gaining understanding and deepening relationships, rather than an opportunity to prove a point or to win. Racism and other "isms" exist, regardless of whether we explicitly address them or not. In light of this, given that conflict about these issues is likely to emerge, we exercise leadership in a different way.

Conflict, Repentance, Confession, and Conversion

When we first began telling stories about our work in youth ministry with adolescents from quite different cultural contexts than our own, an audience member asked Katherine after her talk, "So is this basically a confession?" Ouch. And, yes. This book is a confession of sorts, but we mean this to reflect the best that Christian tradition has to offer in terms of understanding confession as *metanoia*, as repentance that leads to a changing of practice and action in the world. As a Christian practice, confession allows for the naming of sin in an atmosphere of grace and forgiveness. The naming of brokenness, the recognition of historical wrongs and their contemporary manifestations, and the naming of ongoing privilege that is built into our identity is not a fruitless act of self-flagellation. Rather, it is a practice in which we attempt to attune our minds and hearts with God's desire for the world. Confession reminds us that oppression and privilege do not contribute to the reign of God on earth, and serves as a practice of remembering where our hopes for the world are different than the status quo. As such, confession can be an important practice for dismantling inequality.

CHAPTER 3 ————————————————————————————

The Agency of Youth

"The question I have is: Is it better to try to save the whole world, or to work on one thing at a time?" –Casey

THE QUESTION ABOUT VOCATION asked by Casey stands in stark contrast to the question of Andre, who opened the first chapter of this book. Andre's biggest question about his future reflected a concern for the very existence of his life as a young, African American male who saw few avenues for breaking the cycle of violence in the world around him. For Andre, issues of meeting the self and the social world—as we have described vocation—are about sheer survival. This isn't to say that Andre isn't, or shouldn't, be concerned about social transformation as a piece of vocation, but that such vocational concerns arise directly from his experiences of poverty, pain, and violence. This is a spirituality of vocation that starts with the deep material, psychic, and spiritual needs of being a target of violence, powerlessness, and exploitation.

Casey, by contrast, reflects a commonly held middle-class, dominant culture approach to vocation. Casey's statement reflects a stable material environment, so that choosing to attempt "saving the whole world" becomes possible in his mind. Casey demonstrates a confidence in his ability to use his own power to affect change in the world—so much so that his struggle is between addressing injustice issue-by-issue or all at once. In addition, it seems that for Casey, vocation is about something beyond his own reality, a world "out there" which he can play a part in healing.

Andre's and Casey's statements reflect vastly differing expressions of agency in vocational exploration. The contrast in their stories marks the disparities in adolescent males of the same age to have a measure of control over their own lives and to affect change in the world around them. Where Andre demonstrates a powerlessness to preserve even his own life let alone the social conditions around him, Casey reflects the markers of agency, a confidence in his ability to affect change in the world around him.

These brief snapshots into the lives of Andre and Casey help to illustrate how agency is expressed and repressed in the lives of real adolescents. Doing vocational exploration with youth that addresses their ability to have a measure of control over their movement in the world is a complex issue. Additionally, dominant culture resists expressions of agency that challenge the norms of dominant culture. This chapter will explore the ways dominant culture is complicit in inhibiting youth agency, and how the search for youth agency becomes more complicated in settings of multicultural encounter.

The Privatization and Pacification of Adolescence

In order to begin to understand how our youth ministry practices emerged from a particular context, it is important to reflect upon the history of youth ministry as responding to a distinct culture. Such a reflection might help us to more fully understand how our practices of youth ministry may not meet the realities and needs of adolescents from a range of cultural and class backgrounds.

Understandings of adolescence in the US context often inhibit youth agency in the name of preparation for a future life. Young people are not invited into powerful and meaningful participation in the world, rather they are invited to prepare themselves for an imagined future in the economy. Youth agency is further curtailed by the privatization of adolescence, whereby the primary concern for organizing youth activities is to keep them entertained and effectively out of public life.[1] Youth from economically disadvantaged and racially nondominant backgrounds are not well-served by this normative understanding of adolescence—already problematic on face value for the ways it curtails youth agency—because they often do not have

1. Kenda Creasy Dean has written extensively on the church's failure to engage the passion of teenagers. See Dean, *Practicing Passion*.

realistic paths of access to the imagined economic future that justifies the period of extended preparation.

The construction of adolescence that emerged over the twentieth century served to identify adolescence as a liminal space between childhood and adulthood and to privatize the activities of young people into high schools and adult-sponsored youth organizations. Such a privatization of the activities of adolescence, as we will see, has had negative implications for the public expression of voice and vocation for young people in general, and is a particularly detrimental model of youth ministry for working with nondominant youth. As we saw in the case of Andre, adolescence is not always experienced as a leisurely time set aside from the pressures of adulthood.

With the coming of competition for factory jobs at the advent of the industrial revolution, young people were largely excluded from the work force, left to lead public lives free from adult supervision. As historian Thomas Hine describes, "By mid-[nineteenth] century, more than half of the eleven- to fifteen-year olds in the biggest cities were neither in jobs nor in school. If you were a big-city youth who needed some money, you could work for yourself—on the streets."[2] This meant that young people increasingly took on jobs such as courier or delivery services or retail counter jobs. It also meant that kids participated in the darker side of urban street culture—gambling, theft, and other criminal behaviors. The advent of the American high school and of adult sponsored youth organizations such as the YMCA and the Sunday schools were designed in part to keep kids occupied with constructive activities rather than left to fend for themselves on the streets. After the economic downturn of the early twenty-first century, joblessness among adolescents and young people has risen to historic rates.

Religious educator David F. White calls the twentieth century creation of adolescence as a time for activities set aside from the larger economy a "domestication"[3] of adolescence, which continues today as churches and schools pacify youth with trivializing activities that keep them out of public life (and, further, out of the sanctuary on Sunday morning), while at the same time cultivating a vision of future success tied up with competition and economic ascendancy. By creating a vision of preparation toward a future life in the economy, says White, young people are taught to quiet their critical minds, to cultivate skills for winning competitively in order

2. Hine, *Rise and Fall*, 127.

3. White, *Practicing Discernment*, 39.

to prepare for their economic futures, and to spend their time and money consuming clothes, movies, video games and music. White argues that contemporary youth ministry has colluded with the American high school and corporate culture toward the pacification of youth energies, instead of channeling youthful energies toward social engagement motivated by an informed, critically engaged faith.

The Social Location of Youth Ministry

A model of youth ministry that advocates the privatized entertainment and protection of a leisurely class of young people is troublesome because it promotes a culture of privilege and entitlement among dominant culture Christians. If we assume that such a model of youth ministry makes sense for a broader base of youth we may create programs that nondominant youth find irrelevant and patronizing. In reality, many adolescents are hustling to help their households survive economically, something we saw firsthand when the small stipends we offered youth participants in our program were used not for "extras" but to help pay their household's utility bills.[4]

Another common model for youth ministry in dominant culture settings is an enrichment or "concerted cultivation" model, as opposed to an entertainment or distraction model.[5] Middle class families often seek every opportunity for their children's lives to be enriched through extra-curricular activities such as sports or music lessons. In this model, youth ministry often is understood to provide "exposure" to religious understandings for added character-building or spiritual enrichment to an already complete life. In addition to the diminishment of Christian faith to the role of luxury extra, such a model remains primarily relevant to dominant culture families who understand the logic of concerted cultivation as their primary parental role (rather than survival and provision of basic needs, for instance).

---

4. As an expression of our commitment to broaden access to resources for exploring vocation beyond the middle class, FaithTrek offered the three-week, residential summer camp at no cost, and paid an additional stipend to each student to cover three weeks work of lost wages.

5. We have an extended exploration of sociologist Annette Lareau's concept of concerted cultivation in chapter 6. For now, we note that while many critiques of the failings of youth ministry as entertainment or distraction exist, fewer address the collusion of youth ministry models with the middle-class parenting styles that Lareau describes in her work. See Lareau, *Unequal Childhoods*.

William R. Myers, in his book *Black and White Styles of Youth Minis-try*, observed two successful youth ministries—one a predominantly white church in St. Louis and the other a thriving church with a strong African American heritage in Chicago. Myers' work identifies distinct differences between the practices of youth ministry in these churches, a helpful start-ing point for our reflections on youth ministry across boundaries of dif-ference. He describes the youth ministry practices of the predominantly white church as mirroring the dominant culture by creating church as a place for "fun," where the members' middle-class lifestyles are confirmed and guidance is provided to ensure that youth do not fall off track in ways that would jeopardize their economic futures. By contrast, Myers describes the African American youth ministry as explicitly nurturing youth into a counter-cultural African American Christian identity, during which youth take on increasingly public (in relation to the larger church culture) and adult forms of leadership in the church.[6]

Myers points to several important ways that the black style of youth ministry he observed differs from the common practices of white, middle-class youth ministry as we have described them. First, Myers points out that the black style of youth ministry involved much more explicit teaching than did the white form of youth ministry, where the youth group "[has] no real curriculum; often we just sit around and have a good time."[7] There-fore, where youth participation in adult activities in the white church is not expected but is implicitly suggested and invited by adults, the youth in the black congregation were expected to participate in the young adult choir, which regularly contributed to the church's worship services. Ad-ditionally, Myers describes the predominantly white church as reinforc-ing mainstream cultural values including participation in the economic market, and—where the African American church cultivates a sense of group-oriented cultural identity—is concerned with individual morality and growth. Finally, the white congregation in this study mirrors the larger culture in providing spaces for unstructured fun, where the African Ameri-can congregation intentionally builds youth's public activity (agency) and maturation by mentoring youth into adult church leadership roles.

Myers' study of these two congregations—although not representative of either black or white styles of youth ministry as a whole—helps us to reflect more deeply about how the predominant model of youth ministry

6. Myers, *Black and White Styles*, 170–72.

7. Ibid., 150.

that informs the majority of youth ministry curricular resources is built upon white, middle class values of individual enrichment and economic competition. While the goals of economic and personal quality of life are valuable for all persons, they are not sufficient or even immediately relevant to youth without social privilege. For our purposes, this model helps us to reflect upon the ways that our own practice of youth ministry—while it has held a strong commitment to moving youth from the role of passive consumer to a faith-informed public agency—often upheld many of these same white, middle-class values.

Our concern here is that while our explicit pedagogical intent was to move youth from the role of passive consumer to active, faith-motivated agent within creation, we often worked from a one-dimensional perspective on the agency of adolescents, ignoring the ways our implicit assumptions and practices diminished the building of agency for those youth who were not white and/or not middle class. Further, as the people who were in control of creating the program—deciding how to spend our funding, and how to implement the program's curricula—we were in a position of power in this setting. White, middle-class language, practices and values shaped our pedagogical practices, our conceptions of mentoring, and our understandings of vocation, often in ways that subtly re-inscribed our own power and privilege. In the following sections we explore some of these forms of shaping and how they impacted our work.

Entitlement, Cultural Capital, and Agency

We are advocating in this book that vocation is about a meeting of the self and the social world in order to partner with God in God's vision for healing and wholeness. We think that persons must not only cultivate an interior sense of consonance with the divine in which one touches one's God-given goodness and truest gifts, but that one must also have access to the knowledge, resources, and institutions in the social world that make possible expressions of agency and vocation. This, we think, is what the work of youth ministry at its best should be about. It is this access to public life that moves vocation from a privatized, leisurely activity to public faithful engagement in the world.

The challenge to understanding youth ministry as cultivating a sense of vocational identity that can be publicly expressed is that all persons do not enter the process of vocational exploration with equal access to the resources and power structures that make this public expression possible. Such an understanding of vocation presumes that individuals have the access to knowledge, resources, and institutions to express agency and to affect change. Contrary to this expectation, many social theorists have documented how people are socialized into self-perpetuating, unequal roles in society through interactions with family and social institutions (school and church are among the most influential). [8] Philosopher Pierre Bourdieu calls this formation of tastes and worldview created by participation in the maintenance of patterns of inequality "habitus." [9] Our habitus, or our sense of what is valuable in the world and our place in it, is formed by the practices that we unconsciously repeat in predictable and comfortable ways within social systems, even if such practices perpetuate systems of inequality. In some cases, these practices allow us access to institutions whereby we are able build resources for increased privilege. In other cases, these practices inhibit us from accessing institutions that might allow us to increase our well-being.

When we are able to access institutions that help us to build resources to increase our well-being and that of our community, these resources are known as "capital." Every time we are able to build capital—including cultural capital, the skills we develop (such as language) that allow us access to resources and institutions, and social capital, the persons and networks we are connected to that allow for access to resources and institutions—we gain more resources and more skills to gain greater access to institutions that further our well-being.

Education—including public, private, and religious education—is but one among many institutions that have the power to either perpetuate systems of inequality or to disrupt that inequality. By the activities it chooses and the assumptions behind those activities, all educational settings construct activities that can inhibit or enhance the process of gaining cultural capital. In this sense, there is never a practice of education that is politically "neutral." [10] All of our educational practices in youth ministry have very tangible effects on the material lives of persons, for the process of privilege and oppression is reciprocal. As Allan G. Johnson writes, "A

8. Harro, "The Cycle of Socialization," 17.

9. Bourdieu, *Distinction*.

10. The idea that no education is politically neutral was central to the thought of Paulo Freire throughout his works, and picked up and further elaborated by black feminist scholar bell hooks, *Teaching to Transgress*.

group can be oppressed only if there exists another group with the power to oppress them."[11]

Additionally, because persons with access to increased capital gain institutional power as a result of expression of that capital, persons with more power have access to positions of leadership and authority, in education, politics, medicine, church leadership, etc. Among the difficulties that this pattern of acquisition of capital and power brings is that persons with greater relative privilege have a harder time seeing the ways they diminish the well-being of others, and continue to gain additional resources while those who experience the negative effects of this system continue to lose ground. In education, then, this means that persons of privilege who are responsible for setting the context and climate for education make all kinds of assumptions about the level of cultural capital, or entitlement training, that participants should have based on their own experience.

Vignette—by Anne Carter Walker

During a lingering conversation over a cafeteria meal at FaithTrek, I (Anne) sat down with a group of African American and Latina students and staff, who had begun discussing normative "white" language and various forms of vernacular used in specific communities. Tim, an African American teen from inner city Denver, spoke with pride of his ability to use "white" language with adults, in order to keep jobs, do well in school, and generally succeed in the white-dominated world. He also spoke of his ability to shift his language to the vernacular of his peers, so as not to lose face or appear an outsider in his own community. Until this point, I had not realized this shift in Tim's language—that my way of speaking was considered normal and his was considered different, and that both he and I expected that he would adjust his language in order to enter my world and succeed. I carried that conversation for days, further interrogating other aspects of the camp where my perspective appeared the measure by which "others" would succeed. The cafeteria that day served as a borderland of sorts, where we gained intimacy in understanding.

11. Johnson, *Privilege, Power and Difference*, 39.

Language as Cultural Capital

One particular piece of cultural capital in the educational environment— the resource of language and how we use it to communicate with one another— often arose in our work with nondominant youth. The story told in the vignette about an encounter between Anne and Tim sheds light on the complexity of language in the multicultural educational environment. Tim understands that his ability to use multiple languages meant that he could articulate himself toward having recognition of his personhood. He was aware that his ability to "talk white" with bosses and other authority figures had helped him to seek, succeed, and gain greater responsibility at work. With the ability to use the dominant culture's language came respect from Tim's boss, which resulted in more responsibility, which resulted in the building of greater material and cultural capital (e.g., Tim would ostensibly make more money with more responsibility, and be able to relate to a broader range of persons who could be gateways to better jobs, or to college).

This conversation about language came up a second time, when Andre, who was present during the conversation with Tim, spoke with admiration of Tim's linguistic abilities. The context was an interview in which we wanted to hear how the program was going for Andre, how he was learning and growing, and how we might improve the experience for future youth participants. During this conversation Andre noted that we should interview Tim, who was better able to talk on lots of different levels and with different people. While he said this with some admiration, it was clear that he also recognized his own challenges related to his ability to communicate his perspective across lines of difference. He knew that we might fail to understand his insights and perspectives. In further conversation about where he felt he could be heard, Andre pointed out that "dorm talk," which included both the male campers and the adult male staffers talking together during free time in the evenings, felt relaxed and casual; a setting where they could talk honestly about anything they wanted to talk about. This, he said, was in contrast to his nightly covenant group that was run by adult leaders. In that group, says Andre, "We have to say what they want us to say. They don't want to hear what we want to talk about. We have to keep it clean and stuff."

Adults can inhibit young peoples' abilities to speak honestly about their identities, challenges, wounds, and passions—and therefore inhibit the process of meaning making—by assuming that our way of speaking is the most constructive.[12] While discomfort with the "real" language of adolescents might be uncomfortable for us, it is exactly this de-centering of our power and a willingness to take on discomfort that may promote greater reflection and a sense of personal power among the youth in our midst. Because Andre felt he could not articulate his experience fully and instead had to "say what they wanted us to say" in his group, that space was not truly accessible for him in terms of making meaning. Not only could he not speak freely about the content of his thoughts, he also felt inhibited by the nature of his speech. The expression of "voice" is a deeply significant piece of empowerment for persons who often feel silenced and invisible. Without the opportunity for voice, how could Andre fully explore the realities of his everyday life from which his vocational identity must emerge?

This conversation with Andre illuminates a conundrum about cultural capital and oppression. On the one hand, the social agency necessary to affect change in the world requires the building of capital so that one might have access to, negotiate with, and transform centers of power. Tim represents this perspective. He was, in a sense, bilingual. He had the resources to access a certain degree of cultural capital, which, given good mentoring, community support and a whole host of other variables, could lead him to institutions for building even greater capital. At the same time, he held on to his first language, the vernacular of young urban males of color. This is the language of his origin; a private language that shapes his identity and helps him to be sustained.[13] While cultural capital is to be found in acquiring new dominant culture linguistic skills; identity, empowerment and a deeper sense of vocation may not be found in the dominant tongue. For Andre to feel a sense of empowerment, he must also "drink from his own well,"[14] as liberation theologian Gustavo Gutierrez names the practice of drawing on the living water of the wisdom of his community of origin. Vocational exploration starts with the experiences of his immediate life and surroundings, voiced in the language that most fully expresses his identity. To ask him to simply acquire the resources of the dominant culture in order to gain social capital would deny the spiritual and identity resources from

12. Some people claim that we need to make youth use standard English to teach them to "speak correctly," and thereby give them access to institutions of power. I would say, rather, that in our modeling of this kind of speech, we give kids a window into this world, without colonizing their tongues

13. Rodriguez, *Hunger of Memory*.

14. Gutierrez, *We Drink from Our Own Wells*.

his home environment, a deadly proposition. Such an approach denies how this language has shaped his personhood and sense of reality.

At the same time, navigating only in the home language can deny important access to resources, as Andre's experience with trying to express his perspective and ideas to the leaders of the program attests. Educational theorist Lisa Delpit writes passionately about the ways that white, middle-class teachers inhibit the skill-building and empowerment of black children through the use of white, middle-class language patterns. Delpit confirms Myers' study in noting that white styles of speech tend to be implicit and suggestive, where African American forms of language particularly toward children are much more explicit and directive. Delpit explains that white teachers often extend commands to students in the form of suggestions, whereas African American students have been raised in settings where more authoritative, directive commands are commonplace. In such a context, the student sometimes does not interpret the teacher's cues as authoritative, and may respond to the teacher in ways that are interpreted as disrespectful and noncompliant. For black children with white, middle-class teachers, then, the chasm between the implied command and the direct command is so great that the student can be seen as acting out if he does not comply with the teacher's command. Delpit writes:

> Black children expect an authority figure to act with authority. When the teacher instead acts as a "chum," the message sent is that this adult has no authority, and the children act accordingly. One reason that is so, is that black people often view issues of power and authority differently than people from mainstream middle-class backgrounds. Many people of color expect authority to be earned by personal efforts and exhibited by personal characteristics. In other words, "the authoritative person gets to be a teacher because she is authoritative." Some members of middle-class cultures, by contrast, expect one to achieve authority by acquisition of the authoritative role. That is, "the teacher is the authority because she is the teacher."[15]

This mismatch of conversational styles becomes more complicated by social class identity. "Other researchers have identified differences in middle class and working-class speech to children. [These researchers] report that working-class mothers use more directives to their children than

---

15. Delpit, *Other People's Children*, 35.

do middle- and upper-class parents."[16] Middle- and upper-class parents are more likely to veil directives as questions: "Isn't it time to take your bath now?" In middle-class families, both parents and children interpret this language-style as a covert directive. Children who are used to more direct parental commands have been shown to misinterpret veiled directives when entering the school context. "But those veiled commands are commands nonetheless, representing true power, and with true consequences for disobedience."[17] If such patterns of difficulty in communicating persist, where teachers hold the power to decide whether the student is performing adequately and a climate is constructed where the student is repeatedly penalized for behaving disrespectfully, white, middle-class teachers are prohibiting the acquisition of capital by the students for building agency. This subtle holding of capital, represented here in language styles and codes can either inhibit or enhance youth agency.[18]

By holding the majority of the power in the educational context, we as white, middle-class educators were able to set the parameters of relating together, in this case in terms of what style of language would be used, as well as what types of language were permissible in formal learning spaces. Further, because many of the students we worked with came from dramatically different social locations than we do, they did not possess the same linguistic and relational style as we did, and they did not thrive in the settings we created. Rather, spaces are needed that allow youth to speak in different ways. In our experience the arts, worship, and informal spaces for "dorm talk" become important ways to encourage different types of "voicing." We'll explore these issues in further depth in the final chapter. For now, we note that Andre found his visual arts group—where the youth painted murals with images depicting their souls—was a place where he felt he could express himself more freely than in an adult-let small covenant group designed expressly for the purpose of hearing young people.

16. Ibid., 34.

17. Ibid., 33.

18. The tension in this for the white teacher who teaches students of color is that language expressed as authoritative and directive can be interpreted as paternalistic and dominating.

Unauthorized Expressions of Agency

Though we did not always reach our objectives with success, the building of agency by validating the voices and particular life experiences of young people was an explicit priority at FaithTrek. By providing a variety of spaces where youth could express their deepest pains and most sacred longings on their own terms, we hoped that they might begin to connect their inner-most selves with their passions for change in the world around them, and in doing so discover a seedling that might become vocation.

However, many youth were practicing expressions of agency quite on their own, outside of the pedagogical animation we were providing—some-times in spite of us. The unfortunate piece is that we did not recognize these behaviors as expressions of agency, and therefore either ignored these expressions on a surface level or rejected them that which did not "count," epistemologically speaking, as the kind of agency that enlivened voca-tion. These expressions often challenged not only the status quo in society, but also the implicitly-held convictions of our mostly white, middle-class leadership model.

Individual vs. Collective Agency

One of the unnamed assumptions that we carried regularly at FaithTrek was that vocation was largely an individual pursuit. Yes, we thought, an indi-vidual is part of a community, and that community calls out and confirms one's gifts, but it is ultimately up to the individual to respond to the inner voice of vocation. This assumption was challenged for us by a large number of Tongan youth who were present in our program over the years. In a va-riety of important ways, these youth taught us that the making of vocation is not just a meeting of the self and social world, but can be a much richer cultural activity created and cultivated by an entire community. It was the agency that these young people claimed—on their own terms—that made it possible for them to express vocation in authentic ways and for we leaders to learn something about how culture shapes vocation.

Tongan culture, in comparison to mainstream American culture, is more collectivist. The culture of this ethnic group, whose origins lie in the Pacific Island of Tonga, is group-oriented. Allegiance, fidelity, and contri-bution to larger tribe are strong values in Tongan culture. In essence, one's identity is fundamentally intertwined with the identity of the collective. As discussed earlier, we discovered that it was important for the Tongan youth to have touch points with one another, to find space to relax, unwind, and find resonance together.[19] While we adjusted informal interactions to meet this need, we did not make space for collectivist cultural orientations in the larger pedagogical practices of the program. For instance, one piece of the FaithTrek program was that each youth, guided by an adult mentor, would design a practical project that would take place in his or her faith community. The project would be based upon experiences and insights learned during the residential portion of the program, and would address a concrete social need in the youth's home community. While many youth came in groups from the same church, we had two explicit requirements: each individual youth had to have their own mentor, and each youth had to design and complete his or her own project.

The first challenge to our individualist framework came at mentor training. Much to our chagrin only one mentor, Aleah, was sent to our training as a representative for the group of four Tongan youth who would attend the program. As a conversation developed about holding appropriate boundaries with young people (e.g., not being behind closed doors with minors, not driving minors in your personal vehicle) Aleah said, "But these are all my nieces and nephews. How can I do that?" My (Anne's) only response was, "This is a highly litigious society. We have to be careful." We failed to recognize that Tongan culture operates as a large network of extended families. To assume that this mentoring relationship was an isolated, one-to-one relationship in this culture of intricate relationships and family systems, enacted cultural insensitivity even as it expressed white professional norms of appropriate relational boundaries between adults and youth. With deeper knowledge of how to build relationships with young people in Tongan culture, Aleah dismissed my admonitions.

When it came time for the youth themselves to organize a project, they expressed their own agency. They did not complete one project per person. As a collective, with Aleah's support, they planned a series of service projects in their community. The made blankets (a skilled craft in the Tongan community) and donated them to homeless children. They created fundraisers, collected food, and fed the homeless. But, most significantly, they expressed agency in taking control of their own situation, and completing

19. Beverly Daniels Tatum writes: "When one is faced with what Chester Pierce calls the 'mundane extreme environmental stress' of racism, in adolescence or in adulthood, the ability to see oneself as part of a larger group from which one can draw support is an important coping strategy" ("*Why Are All the Black Kids,*" 70).

their project in the way that best expressed their way of knowing, their relationships, and their culture. As a result, their church community saw, for the first time, a group of their own young people mobilized for change in the larger community of Salt Lake City.

These were the first of many important lessons we would learn from the collectivist cultures that were a consistent presence at FaithTrek. We were again challenged to explore our own assumptions about agency and vocation when Telisa, a Samoan youth, shared at a reunion event that she had been pregnant during the program. During the ensuing year, she had carried and delivered a baby who was adopted by her parents. For Telisa, this was fundamentally an act of fidelity and love for her parents who desired another child, demonstrating her place in the collective.

Many times previous to this, the FaithTrek staff had said jokingly how awful it would be if any of the youth turned up pregnant during the course of our year working with them. We said this with a mix of fear about adolescent sexuality, and a sense of fear that we might have contributed to such a "failure" of vocation. What we were expressing were deeply engrained class-based and culture-based assumptions: "Teenagers who have babies are socially deviant and pregnancy is a marker of sexual promiscuity. Having babies as adolescents would invariably lead to school drop-out and potential poverty, and having babies is not a viable expression of vocation."[20] Telisa's particular expression of agency meant that we had to re-consider what "counts" as agential vocation and how the larger collective, such as a network of extended family members, would factor in to our pedagogy for vocational exploration.

Resistance Behaviors as Agency

The expressions of agency that were most fundamentally uncomfortable for us were the many acts of resistance to domination that the youth in our midst were expressing. Sometimes we ignored these expressions of agency as resistance by brushing them off as typical "adolescent behavior," and other times we were deeply disturbed by what appeared to us to be disruptive and

20. Leadbeater and Way challenge this stereotype of teen mothers, stating that while "becoming an adolescent mother can compound multiple, preexisting adversities . . . [becoming pregnant can also] contribute to reduced problems among many young women who are inspired to make something of themselves on behalf of their child" (*Growing Up Fast*, xiii).

disrespectful behavior. These acts of resistance came in the form of sexually provocative dress and behavior, sexually suggestive dancing during camp-sanctioned activities, using swear words and what we considered to be disrespectful language, and wearing sunglasses and earphones in class. What we should have done was to listen deeply to what was behind these acts of resistance, to notice them as "generative themes" that communicate a reality that renders the youth powerless in certain ways, upon which to build an understanding of vocation that takes seriously the problems and challenges of their everyday realities.[21] Instead, in classic white, middle-class style, we were frightened and intimidated by these important expressions of agency, and often used our power as camp leaders to try to suppress these activities—often unsuccessfully.

In response to privilege-based experiences of injury, persons who are identified as "other" or "less than" in social hierarchies often engage in resistance behaviors. By resistance, we mean any activity or attitude that expresses a refusal to be defined by the dominant narrative in ways that denigrate one's self or one's social group. These behaviors and activities can be conscious or unconscious, politically-effective or self-injurious. Resistance expresses a sense of self-worth or self-respect that is not being recognized by the more powerful party, and a desire to self-define rather than be defined by others. When persons are feeling culturally or categorically disrespected, they often engage in acts of resistance that undercut the authority or power that is misrecognizing their worth.

We can all think of protest marches, re-claiming of titles such as "queer" and "black" that were once used to harm groups, and other forms of public and conscious resistance by nondominant groups. However, much resistance is expressed in more subtle and even unconscious forms in day to day experience. Learning to notice such forms of resistance is an important practice for those engaged in boundary-crossing education and ministry. This is one significant site where vocational exploration can begin to address the concrete challenges of the lives of nondominant adolescents.

One of the people who helps us to think about adolescent forms of resistance behavior in a high school setting is the sociologist Julie Bettie. She engaged in an ethnographic study of a high school in the Central Valley of California, and she gives several helpful examples of resistance behavior and the way it is often misread by the teachers in the school. For example, she describes a group of Latina students who decided to be identified as

21. Freire, *Pedagogy of the Oppressed*, 92.

"Las Chicas" throughout the book, and their resistance to the practice of tracking and the hierarchies of status that result from being placed in vocational classes:

> Las Chicas, having "chosen" and/or been tracked into non-college-prep courses, showed little interest in the formal curriculum offered at the school, finding a variety of ways to kill time. They employed rituals of girl culture as an alternative to and refusal of official school activities, including the kind of classroom learning that the prep students embraced.[22]

The resistance expressed in this example is a refusal to be concerned with academics. Bettie notes that this refusal responds to at least two layers of injury. First, the young women (like Telisa) are already functioning in adult roles in their homes, often providing financial and child care support to ensure the survival of their households, and thus resent the construction of adolescence that assumes free time for extended academic preparation for some promised, distant economic future. Second, the school values the college prep students ritually through their award and recognition structures, and fails to recognize the skills and efforts of the students who are combining adult contributions to their households with their school work. Students in the vocational track are forced to attend assemblies that valorize acceptance into college and other academic achievements unavailable to those tracked into vocational classes. Las Chicas ignored classroom exercises and instead engaged in scrapbooking, picture exchanges, discussions of romantic relationship, and grooming rituals as a form of resistance to the norms of the school culture that failed to recognize their material reality. While this resistance behavior was "naturalized" by teachers as typical "girly" behavior, Bettie demonstrates that the elements of class-injury and resistance are occurring with little or no recognition from the adults present.

One practice of class resistance common among working- and under-class adolescents is adopting forms of dress and demeanor that reject the middle class norm of adolescence as extended childhood in preparation for a promised economic future. In Bettie's study, the non-prep adolescent girls often wore heavy makeup and sexualized clothing, thus violating middle-class norms by claiming their adult status "prematurely." She notes, "For them, expressions of sexuality, and by extension motherhood, operated as a sign of adult status and served to reject teachers' and parents' methods of

22. Bettie, *Women without Class*, 60.

keeping them childlike."[23] While Bettie notes that sexual activity was fairly constant across all of the racial and class groups that she studied, only those marked as racially nondominant and working or underclass were perceived as being *too* sexually active. In other words, perceived sexual morality was a site of class injury, as well as a shorthand category used in the place of social class.[24]

When we had the culminating reunion of participants in FaithTrek after four-years of summer residential programs, several of our male and female participants (including Telisa), from three different racial groups but all from working class or poor backgrounds, had become parents. All of them were still in their teens when they took on the role. While we had considered parenthood as a legitimate form of Christian vocation, we had never seriously considered the reality that some of our participants might become parents in the immediate future. This marks again a class-biased understanding of appropriate forms of adolescence that limited our perception of what topics of conversation might be appropriate. Bettie notes:

> Regardless of how a girl becomes pregnant (which occurs for a variety of reasons, including the use of birth control that fails), after the fact, having a baby can be a marker of adult status (just as sexuality was), and girls recognize it as such. For non-prep girls who do not have college and career to look forward to as signs of adulthood, motherhood and the responsibility that comes with it can be employed to gain respect, marking adult status.[25]

Bettie describes how the teachers at the school expressed surprise when babies were celebrated and did not become a source of shame for the girls. The expectation of adolescent pregnancy as a shameful experience lies both in the public acknowledgement of adolescent sexual activity (shorthand for "low class" behavior) and the violation of middle-class assumptions about the norm of extended adolescence resulting in increased economic capacity to provide for children.

What would it mean for a religious educator to "find the spaces of resistance and to join the people in them[26]" in this situation? How might we reject class "liturgies of inequality . . . self-empty [our] practices of affluent taste, bourgeois etiquette, dominant language, and the grammar of privi-

23. Ibid., 61.
24. Ibid., 68.
25. Ibid., 69.
26. Sample, *Blue Collar Resistance*, 35.

lege, and pitch tent with the practices of resistance found in working-class life?" [27] How could we have talked with the young people about the possibilities and struggles of entering the path of young parenthood without re-inscribing class and racial injury through the equation of sexual activity with class status? We may have made the conscious choice not to address these issues because there was no way to do it without being patronizing or without inflicting undue class injury, but our concern is that adolescent sexual expression and parenthood, along with a variety of other resistance behaviors, became part of the unspoken curriculum of our program without much conscious reflection on our part.

In the midst of a culture which would prefer youth to be silent and passive—cultivating skills for future participation in the economy or simply staying out of sight and mind—we find many unexpected expressions of identity and agency, of a struggle to be seen, to be heard, to contribute to family and neighbor, and to survive. Our failure is that, by and large, we did not seize these expressions of agency as the very stuff with which these adolescents might begin to craft their vocational identities. Religious educator Evelyn L. Parker helps us to conceive of a model of vocation for nondominant adolescents that recognizes the integral relationship between spirituality and experiences of injustice. Writing particularly about African American adolescents' experiences of racism, Parker teaches us that spirituality must include a "holy indignation" for the experiences of silencing and violence that so deeply impact their lives. Such a spirituality, she says, requires an "oppositional imagination," one that

> resist[s] one's present unseemly circumstance by envisioning alternatives to the situation. Oppositional imagination is an alternative way of thinking, an alternative worldview that opposes racial domination. . . . [It] means to resist economic, political, and cultural domination, which racism perpetuates, by visualizing a society free of racism. In short, oppositional imagination offers an alternative way of knowing. [28]

Parker teaches us that it is this oppositional imagination, derived from moments of holy rage, in which agency and vocation are borne for nondominant youth. She writes:

27. Ibid., 105.
28. Parker, *Trouble Don't Last Always*, 48.

> Oppositional imagination as a way of knowing, self-worth, loyalty, moral agency, and holy rage can be understood as strategies that encourage black adolescents to expect that God will transform the sites of domination and that black youth will demonstrate a self-understanding that they are agents of God ushering in human equality.[29]

Youth ministry with nondominant youth, at its best, lends an attentive ear—despite positional discomfort on the part of the dominant-culture adults—to such generative themes as the claiming of voice and culture, the expression of acts of resistance, so that the sort of oppositional imagination that Parker describes here might birth confident expressions of identity and vocation.

Youth agency, whether developed in authorized or unauthorized forms, serves a key function in helping young people grow into their full sense of vocation. Attending to the multiple sites of agency development among nondominant youth requires movement beyond typical understandings of entitlement to consider practices of resistance and collective agency in new ways. Often that agency enlivens to fulfill dreams that may be distinctive from those of their adult mentors, a challenge that we turn to next.

29. Ibid., 148.

CHAPTER 4 ——————————————————————————————

The Politics of Dreaming

POLITICS AND DREAMING MAY seem to make strange bedfellows. Dreaming often connotes a space in which anything is possible. In US culture, we like to tell young people that they can be anything they want to be, the sky's the limit. We valorize social mobility and the power of dreams to move persons from one situation into another. However, this kind of unfettered dreaming downplays the reality of formation that occurs in families of origin, educational institutions, communities of faith, and neighborhoods in which young people grow up. While we often point to the media and other meta-cultural forces that have a powerful impact on values, in reality communities of origin indelibly shape the young people who grow up in them. Good youth ministry encourages adolescents to dream "worthy dreams," and yet "worthy" connotes a valuing that is never entirely neutral.[1] In multicultural youth ministry, what counts as a worthy dream in vocational development may differ between the varieties of communities represented.

Older adolescents already have powerful formation into an understanding of the world, what is valuable within it, what commitments are worthy to give one's life to, and other basic elements of vocational dreaming. However, these images of the world, God, and themselves are not yet critically or even at times consciously held. Anyone who has taught adolescents knows that it can be very exciting to walk with young people as they discover that their commitments are not universally held and as they begin the process of examining those commitments in order to hold them more

1. Parks, *Big Questions.*

critically and consciously. However, teaching adolescents can also be quite daunting because introducing them into conversations and communities can cause seemingly (and admittedly, often temporary) drastic shifts in their identity and commitments.

When we work with young people who come from communities quite different than our own, who will be returning to those communities without the immediate power to change their location within them, serious ethical issues emerge. What is the impact of vocational discernment that occurs in communities that look quite different from one's community of origin, particularly when you leave a nondominant community for a dominant one? What responsibility do we have as teachers and youth ministers who don't share, understand, or at times even recognize the wisdom of the young person's community of origin?

The form of education we are hoping to avoid here is what Paulo Freire once dubbed "cultural invasion." Freire described the potentially colonizing form of education in which the values and wisdoms of participants are denigrated rather than taken seriously by those who are teaching: "In this phenomenon, the invaders penetrate the cultural context of another group, in disrespect of the latter's potentialities; they impose their own view of the world upon those they invade and inhibit the creativity of the invaded by curbing their expression."[2] Clearly such a form of education violates an understanding of vocation and agency that allows young people to remain rooted in their systems of social support and cultural heritage as they discern how they might participate in God's work in the world.

Avoiding these colonizing aspects of education calls into question formulations of teaching such as that of Parker Palmer, who notes that authentic teaching means that we "teach who we are."[3] While Palmer's description of the relationship between identity and authenticity in teaching communicates a key idea—we of course do teach who we are in both explicit and implicit ways—we also are teaching what we *are not* in multicultural settings of education. Where teaching who we are has the potential consequence of replicating structures of domination and denigrating the cultural wisdom of young people, the kind of deep humility that Freire advocates for educators becomes even more important. Freire is a helpful conversation partner in education that crosses boundaries of privilege because his own pedagogical method was developed for middle-class teachers crossing into im-

2. Freire, *Pedagogy of the Oppressed*, 133.
3. Palmer, *The Courage to Teach*, 1.

poverished and indigenous communities in Brazil. In the case of vocational exploration with youth, it is important that the teacher is aware of his or her own class-based assumptions about what qualifies as a viable vocational identity, so as not to foreclose for the youth their explorations in images and wisdoms that make sense to their home communities. The complexity of this process lies in the fact that teachers must also be aware that they hold particular cultural capital, and that the explicit sharing of knowledge and resources is necessary in the process of a vocational exploration that is to be both an imaginative process of identity exploration as well as a process of critical social analysis and engagement. Walking the line between sharing access to cultural capital and avoiding cultural invasion will be a constant process of erring on one side and the other. However, naming both potential problems allows educators to attend to their role and signal participants when they think they are engaging in which process.

Multicultural educational communities can be lively places for the recognition of latent commitments and cultural understandings. Being around people with significantly different backgrounds raises the possibility of increased self-awareness in the face of contrasting commitments and cultural understandings held by others in the learning community. Participating in such communities can also be a painful process, as identity-bearing commitments and values get questioned and sometimes discounted by other persons. When this happens in mixed company, the power and politics of dreaming become more evident. Certain dreams and visions of God, the world, and one's role are validated by the broader culture while others can be misunderstood and mislabeled as unworthy or not viable. Less damaging but perhaps equally difficult is that the dreams can just fail to register with others—they are culturally unintelligible across boundaries of difference. Border-crossing education that seeks to stimulate vocational discernment and dreaming ignores the politics of dreaming at its own peril.

Vocational Reflection is Not Just for the Privileged

Before moving on to talk about dreaming alongside young people across the boundaries of privilege, I want to address the notion that vocational reflection is a sort of luxury good reserved only for those young people who have privilege in various ways. Because the idea of vocational discernment implies that young people have multiple options about how they will respond to God's calling in their life, adults working with young people from lower class or nondominant communities may assume that first basic "survival" needs must be met. Often programs targeted to such "at-risk" youth focus on keeping them off drugs or out of criminal behavior rather than attending to the tasks of naming how they see the world and their role in it. We staked our work at FaithTrek on the claim that vocational reflection, questions of meaning and purpose in the world, aren't just for a privileged few. Each young person, regardless of their economic or family situation, their school success or their likelihood of college attendance, should have the opportunity to ask the question of how they might join God's ongoing work in the world and discover a calling within it.

At times, though, we struggled with what vocational dreaming might look like when young people are truly unsure of their survival. To return to the response to our application question inviting participants to imagine themselves at thirty-five years of age, many versions of vocational discernment for adolescents involve long-term planning, college, and career choices. Many of the initial ideas we had about vocational reflection, such as settling into ongoing spiritual practices in community to "listen for the voice of vocation," began to sound a little trite when young people were not sure they would have a future, much less one that they will have some agency in determining.

Some might argue that attending to vocational discernment in the midst of real challenges to survival such as living within a context of violence and inadequate institutional support for education and medical care violates humanist psychologist Abraham Maslow's classic understanding of the hierarchy of human needs. He argued that existential questions (self-actualization in his conceptual schema) cannot be addressed until the basic human needs are addressed.[4] Pastoral theologian Tex Sample might give some credence to this, noting that the "use of introspective practices and an ongoing focus on their own interiority" is valued more by the professional and managerial classes than by working-class people.[5] However, to assume that persons who struggle to survive, who have a hard time gaining access to the resources to meet everyday human needs, do not wonder about questions of meaning and purpose denies some aspect of humanity to persons on the basis of their economic and social status.

The deep irony here is that in order to experience hope rather than nihilism, "a chance for people to believe that there is hope for the future

4. Maslow, *Motivation and Personality*.
5. Sample, *Blue Collar Resistance*, 27.

and a meaning to struggle" as Cornel West names it, some assumption of a future, purpose, and meaning is essential.[6] But models such as Parker Palmer's description of finding life's one true calling, the thing that you cannot not do, didn't really seem to describe the process of what vocational dreaming looked like in the young people who participated in FaithTrek.[7] Rather than finding a vocation that was in some far-off, imagined future, or a sense of true selfhood that could be discerned from the patterns of one's life, the youth seemed to develop a sense of ongoing vocation, emergent, made in the everyday rather than discovered or found. Anne Wimberly links this sense of "hope-building vocation" to a robust concept of liberation in her book *Soul Stories*. She notes:

> Our youth are searching for guidance in making sense out of life. They question God. They struggle with their identities, their social contexts, their relationships, and the things that happen to them. They want and need encouragement, affirmation, and support in their quest for liberating wisdom and at least some notions if not a clear picture of what hope-building vocation means for their lives.[8]

Such dreaming begins in a different place for adolescents without ready access to the systems and structures of privilege. As Evelyn Parker notes, the agency to live into their dreams is not lodged in ready access to cultural capital, but rather in oppositional imagination that allows for radical self-love and cultural rootedness despite the material reality of their lives.[9]

Dreams Deferred, Denied, and Dismissed

Working with other people's children makes the practice of dreaming fraught with judgments and unexamined assumptions about the status of different kinds of work, fears that young people will become unintelligible to their families, and concerns about who influences the dreams of young people. This section explores the problems of dreaming in languages we don't speak ourselves alongside youth who are forging their own paths in the world that begin in places we may never fully understand. We begin by

6. West, *Race Matters*, 29.

7. Palmer, *Let Your Life Speak*.

8. Wimberly, *Soul Stories*, 17.

9. Parker, *Trouble Don't Last Always*, 143.

naming some of the places where dreaming alongside young persons from quite different social locations failed or caused problems. Then we move on to describe some of the potential benefits of dreaming together across boundaries of privilege.

Misrecognition/Failure to Understand

One of the first problems in dreaming with young people about their vocation is simply failing to understand the key elements or categories of meaning that are being expressed because they are not categories or values that are important to our own cultural contexts. In a research project investigating the vocational dreams of participants in the first years of FaithTrek, I (Katherine) interviewed young people about what hopes they and their families held for their lives. During these interviews, I interviewed Sita, a Tongan young woman from the Salt Lake City area. I began to ask Sita questions about how she imagined her life at thirty-five. She mostly talked about her desire to start her own family, to continue to be a part of her extended family, and her desire to have a "laid-back" life somewhere outside of the Salt Lake area, preferably in Hawaii.

As a researcher, I was rather puzzled by her lack of commitment and nonchalance about her own life. As a white feminist, I honestly struggled with her defining herself and her future solely in terms of her relationship as mother and daughter. I kept asking questions until she finally noted that she would certainly be working outside of the home for money, and she had been working hard at school after a difficult freshman year. She had wanted to be a lawyer, but the unsuccessful first year of high school made that impossible, so now she hoped to attend the cosmetology school run by a relative so she could work. I left the interviewed puzzled by why my questions had taken so long to get to her dreams of her adult work in the world and the lack of any sense of commitment to her future, what mattered to her about the world, and feeling like she had been so impassionate about anything outside of creating a family within her extended family.

My lack of understanding of Tongan culture is written all over my read of this interview. Later interlocutors helped me to understand that Sita was describing the values of her community and what was most important in it, as well as offering not small clues to her discomfort with the religious and cultural context of Salt Lake City, and her hopes to move to a community that better recognized her cultural heritage and family structure. Because I could not recognize the value of the family structure, its benefits and limitations for Sita, I could not read the signals she was sending. The encounter was likely of little help in discernment for Sita, but taught me much about my own cultural limitations and impositions as someone with a political agenda for the equality and full vocational freedom of women. The capacity to truly hear young people in the vocabulary and images of meaning they hold dear is not always present, even when you share a common language. Sometimes the barriers prevent a shared understanding.

Class Injury/Judgment

One issue that arose in dreaming alongside young people about their futures is the subtle forms of classism expressed in the way that professional career paths were more readily recognized as a way to live into God's calling than were more working class forms of employment and economic survival. This bias can be seen in my earlier story about Sita and her plans to go to cosmetology school, a dream that as a researcher I did not immediately recognize as a valuable theological calling. In other cases, we feared that young people were being tracked out of vocational possibilities and did not have the social and/or cultural capital to recognize this tracking or its potentially harmful economic effects on their future. Balancing the class-based judgments with healthy suspicion about educational systems that maintain social class hierarchies through tracking meant we were walking a fine line in recognizing and affirming the dreams of young people across social class.

A concrete example of this may help describe the problem. One white, working class participant, Daniel, shared with us his desire to be a school teacher. He described his work in the nursery and preschool departments at his church and how this work brought him great joy. Teaching made him feel fully alive. Because he had learning disabilities and had struggled academically, he had been vocationally tracked at school and was receiving training to become an auto mechanic. This curriculum would not allow him to take the courses that would make him eligible for college admission, something he would need to be certified as a teacher. He valued some teachers who had helped him along the way, and spoke movingly about how he wanted to be the kind of teacher who could recognize students who struggled to learn. He talked about how his youth minister was the only one who recognized his ambition to be a teacher, and how the youth minister had encouraged him to strive for his dreams and not settle on being an auto mechanic. His father was also an auto mechanic, and saw this profession as the most viable economic future for his son. Daniel really loved working with his hands, and he struggled with what was the best life path for him.

In this brief narrative, you can begin to see the struggle between the "home" dreams of Daniel's family and the dreams we more readily recognized in a middle class setting that values professionals. We were very excited about the passion with which Daniel spoke of his calling to be a teacher, and lent ourselves to supporting that dream. Behind this recognition and support, however, are questionable distinctions of class and tricky ground regarding the full recognition and valuing of his home social class context. Were Daniel's father and teachers correct in their assessment of Daniel's gifts and passions, and did being an auto specialist really provide the most promising vocational path for him? Or was this an example of tracking that failed to recognize Daniel's true sense of calling to be a teacher? Could this call to teach not be fulfilled through volunteer efforts in his community of faith and other mentoring programs while his economic future was secured through the practice of auto mechanics? Or was the imagination of Daniel's home setting limited regarding his potential, and our program a moment where his true dreaming could occur, allowing him to move into the professional realm of school teaching?

These questions left us uneasy regarding our role as adult mentors in this setting to Daniel. How did we open up the possibility of living into his dreams of God's calling in his life without denigrating the work that his father did or the dreams his family and home school had for him? The possibility of class injury in denigrating the profession of auto mechanic lurked, as did the possibility of failing to recognize Daniel's leadership gifts and the possibility of his calling as a teacher. No easy answers were available for these questions, but raising them was important in our capacity to serve as good dialogue partners for Daniel as he sorted the possibilities for himself.

Cultural Suicide

In naming the affective costs of formal education, Stephen Brookfield coined the phrase "cultural suicide" for the impact education and critical thinking can have on persons who come from communities who do not share the cultural values of the school setting. Students who enter dominant culture educational settings that value certain forms of thinking about the world risk a sort of cultural suicide in the alienation from their families and communities of origin.[10] While Brookfield is primarily focused on the impact of becoming a critical thinker, the phrase can apply to a whole range of forms of alienation that occur in border-crossing educational settings. First generation college students risk censure from their families for becoming too fancy or upscale because of their college experiences. African American students can be accused of acting white because their academic successes and adaptation to dominant culture educational environments are understood to be culturally located in Anglo-American culture rather than authentic to African American communities.

The potential alienation from context of origin through participation in educational environments is particularly difficult for adolescents who will return to their context of origin after the educational experience. Most adolescents have little power to fully change their current living situation or community setting, and some changes wrought in the educational environment may make them vulnerable to persecution or violence in their home environment. While we want to acknowledge their individual agency and avoid undue paternalism in naming this, the possibility of education as a form of cultural suicide was present for some of the youth we taught. Sometimes this was a less serious issue, such as a young person from a family that was fairly anti-Catholic in orientation falling in love with the experience of praying the Stations of the Cross and purchasing a rosary for home use. While this might have met with some resistance at home, it is unlikely that it would cause acts of violence or serious alienation.

Other changes met with more resistance and condemnation from participant's home environments. Sometimes this meant we received a "What have you done to my child?" phone call. Other times we were not sure exactly what the ramifications were. For instance, later in this chapter we describe a young person who came to question her church's and family's relationship with Focus on the Family and their condemnation of LGBT persons. We often intentionally introduced young people to critical thinking about gender formation and sexual orientation, and at times parents strongly resisted our critical exploration of their religious beliefs along these lines. Our dreams for mitigating oppression based on gender and sexual orientation in the next generation at times clashed with "home" dreams for a faithful orthodoxy to Christianity that drew clear

10. Brookfield, "Adult Cognition," 97.

distinctions on these lines. While raising such questions with adults can be difficult, adults have more power to choose their own communities and are not dependent economically on parents and communities with quite different beliefs. The distinctive values of the educational community and the community of origin could cause real trouble for young people who did not have the freedom to express newly held understandings in their home communities.

Because these value conflicts were often invisible to us in the educational setting, our participants at times were left to negotiate between the two worlds. When we worked to develop ties with mentors in youth participants' home communities, we occasionally experienced such conflicts directly. In one case, a mentor threatened to pull her Baptist youth participant out of the program due to a staff member who practiced pagan spirituality. While the young woman who participated in FaithTrek did not share the staff person's beliefs or practices, she valued her leadership in her covenant group because she was offering skills to the young woman for exploring her own Christian spirituality through journaling and poetry-writing. A vocal conflict emerged between the young woman's mentor and our chaplain on staff in which the mentor condemned the staff person for her beliefs and wanted the young person to leave the program. In this case, the young woman remained silent in the midst of the conflict, choosing later to negotiate with her parents to remain in the program. The chaplain worked hard to hear the concerns of the mentor and to reassure her that the young person had continued to value the Christian beliefs of her home community while at FaithTrek. Such encounters raised significant issues about the contrasting values between an ecumenical graduate theological setting in which diversity of spiritual expression was valued and some of the participants' home church settings where such diversity was viewed as a threat to the piety and even the salvation of participants. In such cases, helping participants name the values of their home community and name the contrasting values at play in the educational setting was quite important, as was helping participants think through how they would interpret their experiences in the setting to their home communities and negotiate any conflict that might arise.

Potential Benefits of Boundary-Crossing Dreaming

Access to Resources and Institutions

Dreaming alongside adults with access to privilege can enhance the ability of participants to "read" the institutional structures of dominant culture and to understand the beliefs and values, positive and negative, that they embody. To return to the case of Daniel, our role might have been providing concrete suggestions for scholarship help, for completing requirements to make college a possibility, and for navigating the admissions maze as a first-generation student would be important concrete skills of "entitlement" that we could provide that might not be as available in his home context. The college-like environment of classes at FaithTrek opened up a potential that he could imagine himself thriving in an academic environment distinct from the structures of the high school setting. Simply feeling "at home" on a college campus allows for a different possibility for belonging in college that was not a part of his socioeconomic cultural background. If sharing information about how such institutions work can be achieved without uncritical acceptance or promotion of their legitimating narratives, access to environments that help interpret such institutions can increase the cultural capital of participants and allow them greater agency to navigate such institutions and the resources they barter.

The real struggle of enabling such access is to do so without undercutting the wisdom and values of young people's home communities. When the positive aspects of entitlement—here understood to mean the self-understanding as one who has the right and capacity to navigate institutions of power—can be learned, participants can choose when to invoke them in their home contexts. One participant, a young man named Johnny, exhibited such characteristics to the approval of his home church community, a predominantly black Missionary Baptist congregation. He told the story this way a year after his FaithTrek experience:

> Everybody can see how I changed. When I came back the pastor told me to go up to the pulpit and talk. The way I just walked up there the pastor said, "Wait. Stop. Everybody look at him. He don't even walk the same anymore." I said, "I haven't noticed." So I went up there, and everybody says I speak differently. They say I speak with production and enthusiasm and stuff like that. I was like, "Wow, I didn't think I had changed that much," but obviously I have.

While the capacity to speak to a crowd with passion and authority was already valued in Johnny's home community, they noticed a dramatic change in his capacity to do so when he returned. In this case, his pastor and home community named and embraced his new manner as their own.

Increased Critical Thinking

In multicultural youth ministry the ability to understand one's home context as part of a wider spectrum and to name which contexts have had cultural dominance is valuable educationally for both young people from dominant and nondominant cultural settings. Beginning to name these dynamics and place oneself within them can disrupt the internalized oppression that names members of certain social groups as individually deficient rather than historically dominated. Critical understanding can also disrupt the internalized entitlement that causes some social groups to assume that their values are universally held and valuable for all social groups. Placing one's experience within broader histories of social relationship helps give broader perspective to that experience and provides opportunities for building communities of solidarity and resistance.

New Possibilities Opened

When a particular cultural context restricts the kind of dreaming available to persons, whether because of class or social capital, gendered expectations, or other forms of limitation, a dominant cultural context can sometimes provide a space where new possibilities for vocational expression can be discerned and expressed. For some of our participants, meeting female staff members who were also ordained Christian clergy was extremely important when they came from communities that did not recognize the ordination of women. This opened up vocational possibilities that are not possible for women within their context of origin. For some young people seeing adult religious persons who self-identify as gay, lesbian, bisexual, or transgendered opens up the possibility of simultaneously living a faithful life and living into their created sense of sexual orientation. For others, recognition that college education is possible through the use of loans and other financial aid programs changes the scope of possible vocational opportunities. Access to alternative possibilities of vocational expression can be a subtle form of domination if they are presented as universally desirable.

But, if we take seriously the agency of young people and honor the values of their home communities, having a sense of multiple possibilities for their lives increases their capacity for making decisions amongst them.

Promising Practices

Vignette—by Alicia R. Forde

Memory is subjective. Given that, I interviewed Jenna to assist me with writing this piece. When I met her in 2006, I made some assumptions. She was seventeen years old. Lanky. White. Thoughtful. From her Faith-Trek application, I knew she sang, played the cello, and had an interest in ministry. From her application, I gathered that her idea of God reflected a theological framework far more conservative than my own. And, oh, she was home schooled. I created a story: one that involved particular conclusions about class, education, and her ability to wrestle with multi-faceted theological concepts.

She was assigned to the Religion and Politics Discovery Group, and her stance was this: "Religion and politics are separate ideas. FaithTrek was a faith-based program. Politics is not faith based. Politics is about debate, and conflict. . . . The two are not connected and they were not going to be connected. Church and politics have nothing to do with each other at all."

I am remembering our trip to the Focus on the Family campus. In our interview, I asked: What happened for you on that trip? Jenna wrote: "The Focus on the Family trip was not good. The whole session and after it. It was the worse [FaithTrek] moment ever. I was raised on Focus on the Family. I was comfortable with it." In fact, Jenna found the campus to be the first time she felt comfortable as a part of the Religion and Politics Discovery Group. Focus on the Family is where she'd received her religious education through their curricula and radio shows. She found meeting their lobbyists difficult—the realization that this faith-based organization had its own political arm. And, the debate that ensued with the lobbyists regarding homosexuality left her confused and unable to figure out for herself what to believe.

My memory of the day's events says that she was struggling. Jenna recalls feeling "in shock and lost." I asked: Knowing all that you knew about me (that I am an out, queer, black, liberal woman who is not necessarily Christian), what made you talk to me that day? She responded: "You were the only one who noticed that I was struggling. Only one who invited me into dialogue, rather than trying to convince me that what I believe is wrong. You didn't try to shove your opinion down my throat."

I've revisited this episode many times since meeting Jenna and staying in touch with her beyond FaithTrek. I have wondered about the role of listening and pastoral care in creating communities of authentic dialogue—even in those moments when we encounter beliefs that differ drastically from our own. Could the pastoral also be generative and deeply prophetic? I have wondered about my initial assumptions about Jenna. What in me conflated conservative theology and lower social class?

And yet, Jenna was the one who seized her own agency and propelled herself through a significant change in beliefs and values. She emailed me almost daily for an entire year—always with intriguing questions about faith, religion, and politics. I watched her shift her position on LGBT issues, and grow into an ally. I watched her move in the direction of Conflict Mediation as a potential vocational choice. Her sense of call to ministry, she says, never wavered. What changed were her beliefs. She says: "I got a sense of the depth of things. My view widened and my call deepened."

Prophetic Listening

Alicia's vignette describes an encounter of nurturing different dreams in youth ministry in ways that honor the dreams and agency of the young person. Working with an adolescent raised in a white conservative Christian community, in her role as chaplain Alicia (a lesbian, Afro-Caribbean-American Unitarian Universalist minister) finds herself the unlikely conversation partner to debrief a visit to Focus on the Family headquarters in Colorado Springs, CO. While full inclusion of LGBT persons in the church is a prominent feature of the conversation, Jenna was struggling in particular with the combination of faith and political advocacy she discovered in an organization that was a prominent feature of her family and church growing up. Another value she had absorbed from her home community was the importance of the separation of faith and politics, which she stated on the first day. The cognitive dissonance created by the visit was clearly disturbing to Jenna, but the interpretations that others offered (she needed to change her own understanding) were not sufficient. From her theological to her sexual orientation, Alicia embodies many identities that Focus on the Family (and by extension Jenna's home community) would not recognize as particularly valuable. Yet, she is one person able to help Jenna sort through her own feelings and commitments about the visit at the site. Jenna identifies the fact that Alicia did not attempt to convert her or to enlighten her, but she was the one person who invited her into dialogue about the encounter, as critical to her own growth and integration.

Alicia describes a ministry encounter as a moment of recognizing the struggle for understanding in the young person and providing a pastoral space to listen to that struggle. While Alicia names her own internal contradictions and shortcomings in the encounter—conflating class status and theological understanding, low expectations for change—her outward interactions with Jenna clearly provided the kind of hospitality that Jenna needed to sort through her own internal contradictions. In true confessional spirit, I should probably note that Jenna felt that no other participant or adult in the community was able to do that for her at the moment. This sense of aloneness points to the limitations of the learning community in enlivening and nurturing different dreams. But Alicia's attitude of hospitality (some might say humility) allows for a space where Jenna can begin to demonstrate her own agency in sorting through the issues raised by the visit.

What is being described in this vignette is not mirroring or unconditional positive regard as a pastoral practice. Alicia is struggling to put words to a different kind of prophetic listening. Jenna knew who Alicia was, and she knew that her exploratory group leader that had designed the field trip and many of her colleagues disagreed with Focus on the Family for any number of reasons—the lack of inclusion of persons of color in the organization (our adolescents of color picked up on this immediately), the gender conserving roles that the organization promotes, the combination of faith and electoral politics that Jenna herself is struggling with. And yet, in that environment, she was able to wrestle with her self-understandings and world view in a way that continued to honor her call to ministry. She emerged from the encounter with greater vocational certainty while shifting some elements of her sense of the world in ways that were quite powerful.

Dreaming on their Terms

Another important element in our capacity to dream alongside young people was the decision to create spaces where young people could dream in languages in which we were not "expert." As a graduate theological institution, words and theological reflection were our stock in trade. In our work with youth, we intentionally enabled spaces for artistic expression, reflective prayer and youth-created, corporate worship where participants could articulate their dreaming in languages we could sometimes hear although they were not our primary mode of self-expression. Once moved into nonlinear and nonlinguistic forms of self-expression, we were not so much the recognized experts. In this way, we hoped to construct a community in which the youth might develop a number of important capacities—personal reflection, negotiations in community, artistic expression, prayer and worship, critical study—to express their dreams for their world and their role within it. For many youth, the Friday night coffeehouses that were a part of the weekly schedule became an important location to share their passions through poetry, song, spoken word and dance. Each of our covenant groups eventually worked in both spoken reflective language and a medium of artistic expression (poetry, visual arts, drama, and music). Also, moving from prose forms of words into poetry and art sometimes addresses the incapacity to hear and the linguistic barriers as staff members found their imaginations were better able to cross boundaries of privilege in non-prose forms.[11]

Vignette—by Kristina Lizardy-Hajbi

One day, a white youth participant named Sarah pulled me aside into the prayer room to talk. She was crying and visibly upset. She shared the story of a fight in her first covenant group meeting in which she and Jared, an African American participant, had argued over whether avoiding "bad" words would be a part of their group's covenant. Sarah explained that she had never spoken to a black person before, that in her school system different racial groups self-segregated to avoid conflict.

11. Another great organization that shares this pedagogical mode is Spy Hop Productions, a not-for-profit youth media arts and education center whose purpose is to empower youth to express their voice and with it create positive change in their lives, their community, and the world. For more info see, www.spyhop.org, accessed 9/14/09.

She was convinced that Jared hated her, and she would not be able to return to the group. I was able to talk through the situation with Sarah, to identify some of the dynamics that were happening in their interaction, and to help Sarah name her fears. At the end of this conversation, Sarah still believed that she was unwanted in the group and would not be able to live in community with Jared and the other participants.

Not until another participant in the group, Melina, a Tongan young woman, dropped by to join the conversation with Sarah did the possibility for connection re-open. Melina, not generally known for her conciliatory gifts, was able to express to Sarah that her presence was valued in the group while still helping to interpret why Jared did not appreciate her suggestion about the morality of using expletives. Without pandering to Sarah or reinforcing her dominant culture values, Melina served as a boundary-crossing interpreter, someone who could see both sides of the experience and bridge the cultural miscommunications and gaps that were occurring.

Boundary-Crossing Interpreters

Another key pedagogical element of the community was the presence of boundary-crossing interpreters who could bridge some of the wider gaps between staff persons and adolescent participants. Sometimes the youth themselves served in this capacity, as evidenced in the vignette from Kristina Lizardy-Hajbi above; sometimes the role was taken by staff colleagues with better insight about the culture of origin who could bridge the distance between the home communities and the educational environment that embodied certain dominant cultural values. Additionally, it was important as an institution for the program to build relationships with adults in the home communities of participants who could serve as boundary-crossing interpreters by helping us to better understand our work with the youth and how it translated back home.

The dreams of young people draw upon the images, values, and desires of their home communities. In multicultural settings of youth ministry, an attempt can be made by adults to dream alongside young people, to recognize their visions of God's work in the world and their possibilities for joining it. At times, these dreams are lost in translation, at other times the intercultural setting allows for better clarification of the particularity and importance of the dreams. Attention to the possibilities of cultural invasion and to the possibilities of failure to engage those dreams adequately temper the potential benefits of access to the structures of privilege that multicultural youth ministry can open up. While dreaming is about possibility, it also opens up a political reality in which differences in power matter greatly.

CHAPTER 5

Negotiating Respect

RESPECT IS A PRIMARY marker of successful border-crossing contexts of youth ministry. Establishing respect takes intentionality, a much more robust process than simply invoking respect as something we intend to do with one another. Respect begins with appreciation, starting with the strengths that each person brings to the relationship. However, in multicultural contexts, appreciation is not always present when relationships begin. At the end of one of my early experiences in residential education with youth, I remember another member of the community saying to me, "When we started, I didn't appreciate you at all." We laughed for a while, as we had clashed several times over deeply held and divergent beliefs. Later, we both could say to one another: "After working with you all summer, now I appreciate you." To really know and appreciate one another can be an acquired perspective, an achievement of relationship rather than a ground rule of it.

When we speak of respect, we are not speaking of easy politeness. Instead we are talking about a robust development of a deep level valuing of the other person, even as they may be quite different from oneself. True appreciation and eventual respect requires time to listen carefully, to understand better where one another comes from, and finally to move into relational respect.

We began the process of establishing relationships with young people through a narrative process in which they reflected on their strengths, their gifts, and their passions. In the prior experience of some of our participants, narratives told about them in school and other contexts were generally framed in terms of their deficiencies and those of their communities. They began descriptions of their communities with "I live in a bad neighborhood" or "I go to a lousy school." To begin with a genuine and appreciative exploration of strengths put us in a position where respectful relationships could grow through dynamic interactions. Sara Lawrence-Lightfoot focuses on this mutuality of respect, by noting that the one who gives respect is also the one who receives it. She also focuses on respect not as a ground rule of community but rather a developmental task of its life together. Respect develops in practice together through the give and take of trust and relationship.[1] Lawrence-Lightfoot describes the way that even in unequal relationships (such as teacher and student), respect can create symmetry and empathy:

> Rather than looking for respect as a given in certain relationships, I am interested in watching it develop over time. I see it not only as an expression of circumstance, history, temperament, and culture, rooted in rituals and habits, but also arising from efforts to break with routine and imagine other ways of giving and receiving trust, and in so doing, creating relationships among equals.[2]

Without respect, boundary-crossing relationships with young people are impossible. However, as Lightfoot-Lawrence notes, cultural expressions of respect vary from community to community, and giving respect often requires fairly sophisticated and careful listening in relationships with persons from other cultural contexts. This means that respect becomes a negotiated gift within communities, where people learn from one another which expressions of respect are meaningful and relevant.

R-E-S-P-E-C-T, Find Out What it Means to Me

From Aretha Franklin's timeless song, we notice that respect may have different meanings to different people in relationship with one another.[3] When my masters students talk about what they need in educational settings in order for productive discussions and learning to occur, particularly

1. Lawrence-Lightfoot, *Respect*, 10.

2. Ibid.

3. "Respect" original lyrics by Otis Redding in 1965, the "R-E-S-P-E-C-T" chorus quoted here was added in the Aretha Franklin version produced by Jerry Wexler and Arif Mardin in 1967.

in settings where there is not cultural uniformity, "respect" is always named as a bottom-line issue. Unfortunately, many of these same students assume that everyone understands what "respect" means and how it should be demonstrated between classroom colleagues. In fact, the practices of authority and respect are culturally-bound; that is, the forms of address, speech, interaction, and conflict that are involved in commanding authority or demonstrating respect vary between cultural contexts. As a commonplace example, in US culture, respect requires that when you want something from someone you request it politely, but directly. In many other cultures, respect requires first engaging in several social gatherings to establish a relationship, and then working through one's mutual acquaintances to negotiate what is needed from the person who has the resource. Direct request is considered disrespectful and rude. However, working through contacts indirectly seems labyrinthine and inefficient to many persons from the US, and potentially ethically-suspect in terms of the history of the practice in "old-boys" networks critiqued in feminist and racial liberation movements. This one example of differences in manner of address, tone of voice, length of eye contact, gift giving, and other embodied rituals of showing and receiving respect points to the many layers of exchange in creating respectful relations.

In multicultural learning communities, it is not enough to name "respect" as an unspoken good. Participants need to live into and learn about the differences in cultural expression of respect. For example, in some cultures respect is always deference. In other cultures, respect can mean taking someone seriously enough to fight with them and challenge their ideas and speech. Respect in multicultural educational situations is always a negotiated commodity. It cannot be easily exchanged without finding out what respect means to the parties involved. When negotiating both generational and cultural differences in a youth mentoring setting with a social history of disrespect in the relations of the groups that different participants represent, the emergence of respect can be particularly challenging.

When Respect Collides with Entitlement

Authority and respect are culturally relevant "adolescent issues" made much more complex in border-crossing settings of youth ministry. The lived culture of adolescent and adult authority, when layered with social histories of inequality when the adults come from more dominant social groups and the adolescents from more marginalized social groups, become tricky to negotiate. Adult educators need to have some recognized authority in order to serve their roles as mentors to young people. However, when the adult authority is combined with a history of race- and class-based injury, the living into such authority is likely to generate as much resistance as learning. If young people sense that the adult leaders do not recognize their situation, their sense of the world, and their cultural values and norms, this appropriate adult authority can shift into lack of recognition and worse, cultural imposition or denigration.

Before I go on, I need to point out that respect is not always a positive commodity. Respect can be code language for continued recognition of entitlement. Many times, the need for respect is emphasized more clearly in cultures that are more hierarchically arranged. For example, in the Deep South in the United States manners of address in conversation, particularly between adults and children, are very clearly enforced. When I (Katherine) moved to Alabama as a high school student, I learned within a day that it was important to use the terms "sir" and "ma'am" when addressing my teachers in the classroom, the parents of my friends, and the adults in my church congregation. These titular forms of address are considered a minimal offering of respect to elders. They are also commonly used by service employees at restaurants and stores as a way of honoring customers.

I had an acquaintance from Canada who confessed that when she first moved to Atlanta, the regular use of "ma'am" in stores and businesses felt oddly formal, even mocking when she encountered it. She said it felt a little like having store clerks say "yes, your highness" every time she heard "yes, ma'am." Her discomfort with this everyday occurrence caused me to begin to think about the function of the habitual use of such titles and why it had been maintained in the South. These greetings and forms of address reinforce the hierarchy of authority. While they are often valorized for expressing politeness and respect (e.g., the icon of the "Southern gentleman"), they subtly serve another function in the cultures in which they are used. They reinforce the hierarchical structures of power in place in the culture.

Perhaps with elders this hierarchy is not such a bad thing. However, the South has a history in which adult African Americans were expected to use these terms of respect when addressing younger Anglo-American adults who would reciprocate with the use of first names, a sign of disrespect. The structures of authority were maintained in the South long after their use was discontinued in the rest of the United States because the careful distinctions of respect and authority were critical to maintaining racial hierarchies. To a lesser extent, their gendered distinctions also maintain gender hierarchies: "yes, sir" always carries more weight for compliance than "yes, ma'am," and it matters that these respectful modes of address are gendered. Another place that such terms maintain their common use is within the military, again a culture where distinctions of power and authority are essential. Lightfoot-Lawrence calls this hierarchical offering of deference the "traditional view of respect" and notices its static and impersonal nature: "Usually, respect is seen as involving some sort of debt due people because of their attained or inherent position, their age, gender, class, race, professional status, accomplishments, etc."[4] The respect "due" someone because of their status or position reinforces rather than undermines hierarchies.

Why spend such a long time delineating the relationship between the hierarchies of power and the notion of respect? At times, charges of lack of respect in multicultural educational settings are actually charges that the entitlement of a certain person, their privilege, is not being recognized as it normally is in other settings. This feels disrespectful to them, and probably is a form of insubordination, though we would not use that term for it. The term "insubordination" describes what is going on in these situations. The assumed hierarchy, the ordering of authority, has been violated by persons in a lower position not recognizing the status of their "betters." When a lack of respect is invoked as the problem in such a situation, I am troubled. Here, "respect" is code language for what are actually practices of deference that maintain social hierarchies of privilege. When the expected level of respect is culturally informed by histories of domination and privilege, charges of disrespect may actually indicate movement towards greater equality and shared levels of authority and power.

Despite the problematic reinforcement of hierarchies related to respect, most people understand respect as an unequivocal moral good in relationships. "Be respectful" is always one of the character education mantras offered to my elementary-aged children in their public school classrooms. If respect is meant to be offered universally and with attention to the variety of cultural forms of showing respect, it can be a helpful value in mentoring relationships. However, my lived experience of respect is that it is often awarded along the lines of power connected to a variety of identity markers, making the demand for respect as a bottom-line quality of the

4. Lawrence-Lightfoot, *Respect*, 9.

classroom or of mentoring relationships not always clear-cut or an un-equivocal moral good. When understood as an achievement of communal life that moves our daily practice together toward mutuality and healing, toward empowerment and self-respect, toward curiosity and attention to one another, respect prospers.

Respect, a "Natural" Adolescent Issue

When "dis" entered adolescent vocabulary as a verb some decades ago, it provided one marker of the importance of respect in contemporary Ameri-can adolescence. Perhaps dis(respect) and respect are particularly salient issues for adolescents because they have adult bodies and emerging adult minds, and yet they are not fully recognized with the status privileges of adulthood. Issues of respect and status, particularly between adolescents, along with "turf" and the other markers of recognition of one's place in the world cut sharply because adolescence itself is an in-between place in our culture. Adolescents are no longer children, and not yet adults. To garner respect is to be assured the recognition of one's worth and importance in the community, to been seen and recognized as valuable despite this in-between status. As such, it is an important piece of vocational development for adolescents.

Some years ago I took a group of twelve high school seniors to meet with the chaplain of a women's prison to talk about compassion and how it relates to the judicial system. My learning goals for the event were three-fold. First, I wanted the young people to meet a professional who was clear about her calling and who by all accounts had been effective in this setting. Second, I wondered if they could meet the inmates and connect compas-sionately with their stories and situations, and begin to think critically about our judicial system and its effects on the lives of real persons. Third, many adolescents (and adults) in our society have never been in a prison, and it is a hugely funded social institution that many people believe in without ever having been in one. So, we spent one morning visiting the prison.

To be honest, I had never been inside of a prison up to that point, and I was taken aback by the rituals of domination that were present in the minute-by-minute lives of the inmates. While I could probably have talked about the prison theoretically as such a place, even invoking Foucault's *Discipline and Punish*, the lived experience of walking through hallways and security gates with inmates impacted me in a deeper, more personal way.[5] In addition to the obvious issues . . . wearing uniforms, walking in lines like schoolchildren, enforced silence, and staying behind locked doors and in small numbers at all times, there were many other subtle forms of reminding inmates of their lack of power. Guards used numbers rather than names to address prisoners. This struck me as particularly powerful when the guard was a young man and the inmate a mature/elder adult woman. I was unnerved by the way dominating power was lived into in this setting.

Later, when we debriefed the day at the prison, the young people spoke movingly of their time with the chaplain and the inmates whose stories they heard. They clearly connected to the inmates with whom we had conversed, and they began to question the drug enforcement policies that had brought many of them into the prison system because of addiction. Throughout this conversation, I was surprised that they didn't name or seem to even recognize all of the rituals of domination/subordination that were a part of the culture. When I began to name the elements of interaction that had fundamentally seemed disrespectful to the inmates, they could recognize them, but the young people seemed befuddled by my attention to these things.

I told the story of the prison visit recently at a conference and expressed my surprise that the young people could not "read" the culture of prison and all of the rituals of domination present there, and described how the youth were unconcerned by them when they were pointed out. A professor at the conference looked at me pointedly and said, "Have you been in an American high school lately?" We had a talk about how very similar rituals are part of American adolescents' everyday experience in school. Everyday practices such as needing to request permission and carry a pass to go to the bathroom, being spoken to directively with little tolerance/respect for your input, having other people determine what you are allowed to wear and when you are allowed to speak, or having very little opportunity to shape the curriculum, rules and regulations that are imposed upon your community are regularly occurring experiences. While it is a cliché for adolescents to describe high school as a prison, the two institutions do share some characteristics when it comes to the expression of power through rituals of respect and authority.

Because most adolescents spend their school hours in very large institutions that need to move large numbers of people through predetermined

5. Foucault, *Discipline and Punish*.

patterns of interaction, they tend to emphasize control and respect through rituals of domination. While we often talk about disregard for authority as a "classic" adolescent form of expression, the reality is that our institutions and forms of education make respect and authority a huge part of their day-to-day existence. The fact that adolescents, often with adult bodies and emerging adult cognitive capacities are held in a state of extended preparation for adult life pushes this issue culturally for all American adolescents. It is not "naturally" or "universally" an adolescent issue, it is a product of their day- to-day existence. The lack of respect is amplified when combined with social histories of race and class that denigrate persons from particular racial groups, recent immigrants, or working or poverty-class families.

In thinking about high schools and prisons, I am invoking the issue of respect between adolescents and adults who have authority over them in various institutional settings. This reality impacts the issue of respect on a horizontal plane between peers as well. Living without authority and respect from the adults with whom they interact causes the demand of respect from peers to escalate. Additionally, where young people are identified as members of groups that are broadly disrespected by dominant culture (young African American males, transgendered youth, first and 1.5 generation immigrant youth, American Indian youth), peer respect becomes more important. The search for recognition and status as a human being in the midst of general disrespect from the culture carries the weight of an ongoing lack of respect in the broader culture.

Vignette—by Yvonne Zimmerman

I had carefully laid my plans for covering the topics of gender, race and class in my Discovery Group on Power and Marginalization during the summer session. We started with socio-economic class, but by the time we got to the topic of race in week two, it was quite possible that I had already learned more than the youth I was supposed to be teaching.

To be clear, there was nothing wrong with the youth. In fact, there was a lot right about them. For example, they were incredibly gracious. Take week one: I had this nifty group exercise that was supposed to teach them about socio-economic class. The students lined up in the yard outside and I read a series of statements, like "My parents or I know how to order in a nice restaurant." The students for whom that statement was true were supposed to take one step forward.

But then there were the other statements: "My family knows how to get and use food stamps or an electronic card for benefits." True? Two steps back. "I know how to keep my clothes from being stolen at the laundromat." True? Another two steps back. "I know which churches and sections of town have the best rummage sales." True? Two more steps back.

I watched, horrified as two youth kept moving farther and farther back from the starting point, as the rest moved slowly forward. Even though I was the one in control of the game, I felt helpless because I was doing this to them—essentially calling them out. Why had I not anticipated this disparity? And why hadn't I thought to protect them from this kind of exposure?

Frankly, I have no idea if the youth learned anything helpful about social class that day, but I haven't been able to forget it. I got it—I really got it: Just because they wear the same clothes and listen to the same music and enjoy doing the same things doesn't signal social equality. They start out in all sorts of different invisible paces. I was ashamed, because I had read enough books—I should have known that.

Needless to say, I was more than happy to leave the issue of class behind and to turn our attention to race. I was excited too, because one of my professors, Dr. Edward Antonio, was coming to share with us his life story of growing up fending for himself on the streets of Zimbabwe during its years of civil war, teaching himself to read, lying about his high school education to receive a spot at a local college, going on to university in England, and eventually coming to the United States.

But as Dr. Antonio began to speak, it looked to me like Zach wasn't having it. Zach was one of two African American youth in the Discovery Group, and he was also one of the students whose lower class credentials I had put on full display the previous session. He sat through Dr. Antonio's presentation detached—eyes closed and giving every appearance of having fallen asleep.

I felt frustrated. Admittedly I was frustrated first with myself for my thoughtlessness the day before. But as I watched him appear to snooze the morning away, I became frustrated with Zach, too, because I hadn't messed up the topic of race. I hadn't presumed that as white person I was in a position to teach him the meaning of racial inequality. Moreover, as Dr. Antonio shared his story, it was pretty difficult to miss that the entire first two decades of his life literally had been defined almost completely by racial inequality. From where I sat, this behavior was incredibly rude to our speaker.

As unobtrusively as I could, I tapped Zach on the shoulder and asked him to wake up. This lasted approximately two minutes, and his eyes closed again. Still embarrassed, I let him go.

I spoke with Dr. Antonio about Zach afterwards, apologizing. Dr. Antonio spoke gently, "I saw what he was doing and I can see why you were upset. But I watched him. I don't think he was sleeping." I was incredulous: "Really?" "No," he said slowly, "I don't think he was. I think he was listening. But I think that in order to engage, he needed to shut down. Sometimes staying visibly engaged is just too much." He needed to shut down in order to engage. That's not so crazy, nor was it rude. I could get that. Zach: 2 Yvonne: 0. I may have been hired to teach the group, but pretty much every day, Zach was the one teaching me.

Respect and Resistance

This powerfully honest vignette from Yvonne Zimmermann is helpful because it makes a link between three essential categories for our attention in boundary-crossing youth education and mentoring: class-, race-, and other privilege-based injury; resistance; and respect. These three concepts name important intertwined issues that impact the practice of border-crossing education with young people.

Yvonne initially describes an educational activity that was meant to help young people understand how social class shapes privilege and oppression in everyday experience. What she discovered as she lived into the exercise was that it singled out two members of the group in a way that potentially could cause an experience of class injury or at least re-injury . . . an unmasking of previously hidden distinctions that sorted the group into those who are normalized and valued by our culture and those who are denigrated. In the setting for which the activity was designed, these class-based differences would likely have been much more mitigated. However, in an environment with persons from multiple social class locations represented, the stark distinctions became quickly and painfully clear. Because Yvonne is a thoughtful, humane teacher, she became dismayed during the exercise because she realized that what she was doing was potentially harmful to the students involved.

The exercise made this experience of class injury particularly clear, but many times when we teach or mentor we don't recognize the small humiliations and distinctions that we invoke that can cause privileged-based injury to our students. We assume that young people have enough to eat at home, or that they know what a mortgage is. We assume that their deepest worries are who is attracted to them at the moment and what they are wearing, rather than whether their family can keep the electricity on or whether they will be assaulted for violating norms of gender performance. We unthinkingly use common metaphors in our speech that denigrate conditions of disability or sexual orientation. We consistently mispronounce unfamiliar names or avoid using them because we are afraid we might say them incorrectly. Most of the time, these kinds of subtle social injuries go unnoticed by persons who identify with the various dominant identity markers who inflict them, but can be alienating and harmful to those who experience them, particularly when they must navigate institutions on a regular basis that are designed around the assumptions and values of dominant cultural narratives. In response to these privilege-based experiences of injury, persons who are identified as "other" or "less than" in social hierarchies often engage in resistance behaviors.

Often resistance is perceived by adults across boundaries of privilege as disrespect or insubordination. In Yvonne's vignette, she confesses a misrecognition of costly engagement in a classroom discussion that painfully names a student's reality. Again, the resistance expressed by Zach is subtle and easily misrecognized: he closes his eyes and appears to be sleeping. Given that Zach had many experiences of school as a place of racial and class injury, the classroom is a difficult place to immerse himself. By closing his eyes and appearing unconcerned, he is resisting the assumption that the classroom space is a place that might describe his reality in any meaningful way. At the same time, Professor Antonio was able to discern the subtle markers of engagement and attention. This form of resistance was perhaps unconscious on Zach's part, and certainly could have been self-defeating, causing him to be removed from the classroom or sanctioned in some other way. At the same time, it allowed him to hear the speaker on his own terms and without fully investing in a space that had already been a source of some injury.

These stories point to the importance for those engaged in multicultural education and mentoring to practice "reading" behavior for class-based injury. What comes across as disrespect on first read may actually be a form of resistance designed to protect oneself against the possibility of further injury or the perceived sense that the educational direction will create boundaries between oneself and one's community. Dealing productively with resistance will be a skill important to any youth leader working with youth from other social locations.

Unfortunately, privileged persons are often taught to respond to resistance through a display of institutional and personal power. When students act out, we sense that we should have been more "in control" of the situation. Such a response towards greater control generally produces more concerted resistance. A more productive response to this form of resistance is to recognize it and lend our energy to opposing the demeaning rituals of inequality that evoke it.[6] While we shouldn't join in practices of resistance uncritically, it is important to choose to position ourselves with nondominant people in practices of resistance to such injustices in concrete and embodied ways where we can. The worst choice we can make is to fight against or punish such resistance, which means to join the dominant culture and become identified as part of the problem.[7]

Negotiating Respect without Domination

Entering a multicultural educational setting from a place of privilege requires careful negotiation to be culturally intelligible and authentic without reinscribing practices of domination. While any educational endeavor requires some form of authority in the role of teacher, and any youth mentoring requires that adults maintain appropriate adult authority, what that authority looks like and what respect for the learner looks like requires careful negotiation when the default modes of adult authority collide with historic patterns of domination. Adults demanding respect may increase practices of resistance if they remain unaware of the histories of injury that inform their current relationship with young people.

An example of where negotiating such respect became necessary and painful in our program occurred one summer in several interchanges between a few adult white women leaders and a few African American male

6. Sample, *Blue Collar Resistance*, 62.

7. Ibid., 11.

adolescent participants. The adult leaders felt that their authority was being ignored and they were being treated disrespectfully by the adolescents. The adolescents felt that the adults were afraid of them and overly restrictive in their control of their behavior. Both parties felt injured by sexism and racism in the interchange. There was a sense of uneasiness and perceived disrespect from both parties.

At least four factors were at play in this relational difficulty:

1. White women leading with authority in forms that teens did not recognize

2. Adolescent anti-racist, anti-bourgeois resistance behavior to authority in educational situations

3. Normative sexism in music and other cultural forms familiar to the adolescent males that were informing their speech

4. Social histories that make relationships between African American men and white women particularly fraught and over-determined

The complexity of all of these factors (race, class, and gender) played heavily into the interaction. After several incidents were privately discussed among the parties involved, the issue was raised in a way that led to conflict among staff, who tended to talk about one or the other elements in working through the situation. Again, what could be summed up as a simple "lack of respect" in the relationships really addresses whole histories of inequality, entitlement, and race- and gender-based injury. To name disrespect as the problem and enforce entitlement on any one of these lines of history without naming and addressing the others can merely replicate domination against one group in the service of ending domination for another.

While the easiest thing might be to say "everyone has to be respectful;" without recognition of the histories and what is at stake for all parties, enforced respect merely re-inscribes patterns of domination. We need to be explicit about how respect and disrespect are expressed and then come to negotiate how we will be together in community. All of this takes time and can generate conflict because it brings up painful histories of injury and oppression. Such negotiation runs counter to normal practices between adults and adolescents in each context, and as such may be resisted by the young people. Often, when we engaged in such conversations, adolescent participants tended to say "just tell us what our punishment is and let's move on." Some adults also wanted to just sanction the young people and get them to toe the line and offer respect. The process of negotiating how respect will be demonstrated through the day-to-day interactions of the learning community and mentoring relationships is an important part of the journey towards respectful interaction.

Respect may not always be expressed through equal behavior. In the multicultural, multigenerational communities in which we have participated, there has been flexibility within the community on naming practices, for instance. The young people tended to call Anglo-American adults by their first names and African American adults by a title of respect and their first or last name depending on their preference. This decision for unequal treatment achieves two respectful learning goals. The practice of using titles of respect, particularly for African American elders, counters historical practices of domination that denied such naming. Using first names with Anglo-American adults allows for practice in the education for entitlement, learning skills that will allow young people to navigate institutions of power where they live into the role of equality with persons with institutional power. Respect does not always mean equal treatment, but practices of inequality should be carefully examined to be sure that they run counter-directional to historical trajectories of domination.

Second, all parties have to coach themselves not to understand disrespectful behavior as indicators that a relationship is broken and should be ended, but rather as a need for renewed conversation and negotiation. This requires a level of relational intensity and commitment that is often not present in educational settings, volunteer mentor relationships, or even in many familial settings. However, for true respect to emerge among persons in a mixed setting, such practices are necessary to get beyond mere formality and move into the opportunity of true valuing and respectful behavior for all persons involved. Because mistakes will be made, practices for adjudicating conflict and rituals of forgiveness will also be necessary to allow for the kind of mutually respectful relations to emerge.

Mentoring and Eldering

"Those who authentically commit themselves to the people must re-examine themselves constantly."

-PAULO FREIRE[1]

RELATIONSHIPS WITH TRUSTED ADULTS are a key element in youth development work and youth ministry. The nature of interaction between youth and adults considered appropriate varies greatly across boundaries of race, class, nationality, and even region. For instance, as explored in the previous chapter, what should an adolescent call the adults who work with them in a multicultural setting? In some communities, adults always receive a title of respect, prior to either first or last name usage (Mr. Jim or Mrs. Rogan). In other communities, using first names across the generations is considered respectful (Ray or Lisa). In some communities, adults regularly have a familiar relationship with the young people they mentor, and they are addressed with a familial role title (Tío or Auntie, for example). In other communities, adults of different generations are addressed differently according to what was considered polite when they were growing up. Behind these simple changes in form of address lie complex understandings of authority, power, respect, and the correct manner of relationship between adults and young people. While in every instance adults who work with youth care about the young people and hope to contribute to their maturity and development into responsible and caring adults, how one goes

---

1. Freire, *Pedagogy of the Oppressed*, 42.

about this form of eldering or mentoring varies greatly from community to community.

In multicultural educational ministry with youth and young adults, the presence of a variety of ways that adults and adolescents normally interact in their home communities can be challenging. These distinctions in how young people and adults interact are often engaged instinctively rather than consciously. Forms of address and body posturing in relationships between children and adults are embodied behaviors learned very early in life. While these relationships are often being re-negotiated as children move into adolescence and adulthood, their initial format remains powerful well into adulthood, particularly with adults at least a generation older. Adults wield authority with young people in the embodied forms that are normal for their context, but what is normal in one context can seem unduly harsh or permissive in other contexts. In cross-cultural and intercultural contexts, relationships between young people and adults from different cultural contexts must be negotiated carefully if they are to contribute to the agency and flourishing of young people. Without attention to the cultural distinctions in forms of interaction between adults and young people, such relationships can fail to function in a variety of ways ranging from polite distancing to all-out power struggles.

While adolescents from nondominant communities often have experience with adults from dominant communities in positions of power over them, they sometimes have not been given the opportunity to think carefully about those relationships and how to navigate them. The respect of elders may be an expected and natural response to adults in their own community, while a healthy mistrust of adults from other communities may have been intentionally or unintentionally socialized by their elders or by their experiences in dominant communities. If the respect of elders is offered in a dominant workplace setting, it may be misinterpreted as immaturity or lack of decisiveness. A mistrust of authorities performed in a dominant-culture setting may come across as disruptive or "not being a team player." Mentoring relationships can replicate all of these dynamics unhelpfully if they are not engaged critically and with practices of self-reflection on the part of both the mentor and the mentored. In this chapter, we will explore how these cultural assumptions can hinder strong relationships when they are not engaged thoughtfully.

Mentoring across Boundaries

In our residential academic enrichment program for youth, each participant selected a mentor from their home community with whom they established a year-long relationship. This aspect of the program mirrored many other mentoring programs in which occasional pairings found great success. When the adult and adolescent connected, participants spoke eloquently about the power of their relationship in their formation and growth. However, other adolescents were disappointed by absent mentors, or mentors who did not seem to take the same level of interest in them as those of their peers in the program. Sometimes this reflected the individual who had volunteered as mentor simply dropping the ball on their commitment. Other times we wondered if something were missing in the ways mentors were recruited, trained, and supported. Year by year, the staff devoted considerable time and energy in training mentors, outlining clear expectations for the role they could play, encouraging them by talking about how important their role was, providing resource guides for mentor/youth meetings throughout the year, and making phone calls to check in on mentors. Still, the problem persisted that many mentors did not seem to invest the desired energy in relationship with the young people. Such a situation could easily be written off as part of a larger cultural problem, in which adults seem to have little faith that adolescents want or need their presence in their lives and therefore are reluctant to invest themselves in young people. We also wondered if perhaps we had set up an adult/youth relational model that didn't make cultural sense to many of the adult volunteer participants.

In addition to the failure of volunteer mentoring relationships, conflicts about the appropriate relationships between adults and young people can also arise with professionals working directly with adolescents in mentoring relationships. When staff and adolescent participants in an educational setting come from many different cultural backgrounds, disagreements can occur between staff persons regarding the appropriate way to lead, discipline, and advise young people in a given setting. Additionally, both youth and adults occasionally misread attempts at guidance and respect because of the differing cultural codes around how adults and youth should be in relationship. In operation behind these conflicts are varying normative understandings of responsible and respectful relationships, generally unarticulated and yet fully embodied.

Adults as Mentors

As an overall conception of educational relationships between adults and adolescents, we drew on liberative models of education that emphasize the development of agency and imagination in young persons. While the initial proposal for the program focused on relationships with "properly equipped elders who can assist in the development of a holistic vocational identity," we eventually settled on the term "mentors" for the adults from the home communities of participants. In our internal conversation about appropriate relationships between adults and adolescents, we tended to use language such as "partnering with youth," "empowering youth," "inviting youth" and "hearing youth into speech." All of this language mirrors the Freirian pedagogy that also initially informed the shape of the program. In this educational model, young people are understood as persons who have the ability to name the world and become constructive players in it.

Because of the Freirian influence, our language about youth tended to downplay any hierarchical relationship between adults and adolescents. While the staff understood that our relationships with adolescents required appropriate boundaries and should never be collapsed to a peer-to-peer model, there was always an element of mutuality evident in the language about the relationships between adults and young people. For example, one of our mentor training handouts indicated: "The mentoring relationship should be one of mutual respect, growth and guidance. In any mutual relationship, both parties are bound to show care and respect for the other."[2]

In part, this emphasis on mutuality is offered as a corrective to a situation described well by Maisha Handy and Anne Wimberly in their discussion of mentoring youth in the black church. Handy and Wimberly describe mentoring that devolves into monitoring: "criticism and condemning that has created a big generational gap that the church is having trouble bridging."[3] Whereas monitoring emphasizes the power distinction between adults and adolescents, often focusing on keeping youth busy and out of trouble, mentoring evokes a sense of being connected more directly for the learning of the young person. In our design for mentoring, we invited adult volunteers to commit to meet regularly with the young person, to serve as an advocate for the young person and a translator of their educational experiences to the home community, and to help guide youth in the creation

2. FaithTrek 2004 Handbook: FaithTrek Mentors.
3. Wimberly and Handy, "Conversations on Word and Deed," 122.

of a community service project in which they could express their passions to help shape a different kind of world.

The kind of mutual relationship we envisioned for youth and their mentors is evident in the following description of one of their first official acts together: "Utilizing the method of Appreciative Inquiry, mentors interviewed the youth about their experiences and discoveries at the Summer Community and the youth interviewed mentors about vocational gifts they could offer the youth. Based upon these interviews, the teams had time to dream about projects that could be carried out in the coming year." One can see the structural reciprocity and sharing of wisdom that this assigned task intends to evoke. Another handout on mentoring indicates that mentors should "Share important aspects of your life with your youth, and welcome questions about relationships, meaning, and purpose—without judgment."[4] The "without judgment" language indicates the extent to which we asked mentors to leave a parental or eldering sense of relationship at the door as they embraced a more mutual relationship with young people.

From the very beginning, we had concerns about the mentoring relationships. We felt that many mentors were having a difficult time connecting with their youth and completing the planning process for projects. Our response was to offer more detailed information about the responsibilities of the mentor and to try to find ways for the faith community to ritually commission the relationship to affirm its importance. At the time we did not begin to question whether this mutuality was a culturally-bound expectation between adults and youth that might hinder the formation of strong and formative bonds between them.

Adults as Elders

The slippage between the terms "elders" and "mentors" in the development of the project turns out to be a significant indicator of the multiple cultural forms of relationship between adults and adolescents at play in the model. Two of the creators of the project, Rachel Harding and Anne Carter Walker, worked out of cultural contexts (African American and Cherokee) where "eldering" is a more apt descriptor for appropriate relationships between adults and youth. The shift to "mentoring" and the kind of relationship that we structurally assumed between adults and youth through the activities

4. FaithTrek Handout: What is Mentoring?

we designed reflects a predominantly middle-class, Anglo understanding of relationships between adults and adolescents common in youth development literature and social service programs. In mentoring, the focus is on the adult and young person working together for the benefit of the young person. The mode is a "trying-on" of a more mutual relationship, with the adult conversing with the adolescent "as if" they were an adult. While both parties are always aware of the distinctions in power and authority between them (it is mentoring rather than buddies), the pedagogical assumption behind this form of mentoring is that by modeling a more mutual style of interaction, the adult begins to evoke more adult-like interaction from the young person. Thus, the young person's agency is enlivened through the relationship in which "adult-like" interactions are engaged.

The description of mentoring offered by Anne Wimberly and Maisha Handy, both African American educators who work with the Youth Hope-Builders Academy, another academic program for the exploration of vocation with youth program based at the Interdenominational Theological Center in Atlanta, GA, offers a contrasting view of the appropriate roles of adults. In her introduction to the book she wrote about this work, Wimberly notes the importance of mentoring: "Our youth need our presence with them, and the knowledge, insight, counsel, and nurture that come from wise adults. And they are looking for adults who are willing to commit to being involved in their lives on a consistent basis."[5] While using the same word, "mentoring," Wimberly and Handy meant something qualitatively more hierarchically authoritative than our model. They describe a relationship more similar to "elders" rather than "mentors." In eldering relationships, the adult and youth engage together for the benefit of the young person. However, rather than conversing "as if" they were an adult, the pairing is created for the passing down of "insight and counsel." Even in peer mentoring situations, the kind of relationship envisioned includes much more directive behavior than was understood in our mentoring model. Handy also notes: "I think that our churches must also help young people to mentor one another, because a lot of times they can receive correction and advice from their own peers better than they can from an older person."[6] The words "correction and advice" signal a more hierarchical sense of authority on the part of the mentor with relationship to the mentored.

5. Wimberly, *Keep It Real*, xxi.
6. Ibid., 122.

A predominant model in the African American community is receiving "Counsel from Wise Others," as Trunell Felder names it.[7] Whereas our mentoring model advocated being a companion for the journey who listens the young person into speech, these models understand mentoring as offering sage wisdom and living with integrity before the young person. In describing mentoring among adult women in the Black church, Wimberly and Handy use the image of a wisdom guide imparting knowledge by word and deed: "The wisdom guide is the confidante who offers guidance, provides insights, gives feedback, maintains the integrity of the relationship, and models exemplary behavior and commitment to the spiritual growth and well-being of the seeker."[8] This eldering is designed to pass essential information from one generation to the next, wisdom about survival and flourishing through word and action. As such, it is offered with enormous respect and compassion for the next generation. However, respect and compassion are not communicated through rituals of mutuality or shared projects. Rather, elders are to offer with authenticity the wisdom of their life experience in direct ways. As Anthony Reddie describes in his own cross-generational work with African Caribbean young people in Britain: "The work connected younger and older generations so that the wisdom found in the oral tradition of the elders could be shared."[9]

Interestingly, Reddie wants to shift the cultural norms of mentoring within his own community to more shared reciprocity. Therefore, knowing this is against the cultural norm of his context, he provides explicit processual instruction and guidelines, and engages in cross-generational dialogue with a professional educator present. "By inserting these guidelines, it is my intention to ensure that children are (1) heard, and (2) their insights are accepted as valid."[10] For such connectedness and reciprocity to occur, Reddie asserts the importance of "homogeneous" and "compact" community as the location for such sharing:

> Even where there are known generational differences, the existence of cultural commonalities such as physical traits, colloquialisms, and other mannerisms will be recognized and will provide a means of connecting. Commonalities offer an essential starting point for conversations, which allow for cross-generational sharing

---

7. Felder,"Counsel from Wise Others," 89.

8. Wimberly and Handy, "Conversations on Word and Deed," 109.

9. Reddie, "Forming Wisdom," 57.

10. Ibid., 71–72.

of proverbial sayings, cultural historical information and values, and emerging ways of living that call for reflection on wisdom.[11]

While Reddie had similar concerns for reciprocity, as an insider in the community he had greater moral authority to call for it in these culturally homogeneous settings. Given a more diverse setting and the fact that our leadership in mentor training largely self-presented as Anglo, we had much less authority to challenge the latent cultural models of adult/youth relationship already present in the young people and adults with whom we worked.

The emphasis on mutuality in adult/youth relationships as a means of increasing agency seems to be a culturally-specific practice to middle-class Anglos. Many other cultural groups find that agency is better gained through a respectful mode of interaction between generations where the elders share collected wisdom with the younger generation. For example, Joan May Cordova notes that in Asian Pacific American communities, a much more hierarchical relationship with adults (particularly parents) is more common:

> Parents' words are not to be taken lightly, because filial piety (respect for one's parents and elders) is one of the most important traditional Asian values. Sons and daughters show respect for their elders by addressing them with designated words of titles of respect, by being obedient, by deferring to their wishes, and by working hard to fulfill roles and expectations of the family.[12]

In such a setting, activities that demand that young people take the lead in speaking and the adults take the lead in listening can violate cultural norms of filial piety. I want to be clear that the Anglo version of mutuality doesn't communicate more love for or desire for agency in the young. Simply put, it is a distinctive, culturally-specific strategy for achieving it.

Social Class Distinctions in Adult/Youth Relations

Another layer of analysis of the struggles of the mentoring aspect of our program could be that it drew primarily on middle class understandings of the appropriate relationship between adults and adolescents.[13] In fact, our

11. Ibid., 72.

12. Cordova, "Historical and Cultural Context," 32.

13. To focus on class in this section courts the problem of speaking about class in

most successful mentor/participant pairs across racial groups were often ones in which the mentor was a teaching professional or clergy member or where both mentor and participant were from middle class settings. Sociologist Annette Lareau engaged in a study of parenting styles across social class groups and articulated a "dominant set of cultural repertoires about how children should be raised." She noted: "[T]here is little dispute among professionals on the broad principles for promoting educational development in children through proper parenting. These standards include the importance of talking with children, developing their educational interests, and playing an active role in their schooling."[14] Lareau demonstrates how this professional consensus closely mirrors middle-class parenting styles across racial groups in her ethnographic study of parents of elementary age schooling, naming the style *concerted cultivation*. In the concerted cultivation model of parenting, parents share a cultural logic that primarily understands their children as a project to be developed through actively assessing and fostering talents, skills and opinions.[15] Our vision of appropriate mentoring clearly grew out of the cultural logic of concerted cultivation. We asked mentors to listen to the dreams and opinions of the young people, and to assist them in completing a year-long project designed to further develop those talents and visions that the young people identified as central to their vocational journey.

However, concerted cultivation was not the primary style of parenting engaged in by the working-class and poor parents in Lareau's study. Rather, they participated in a cultural logic of child rearing that the sociologist dubbed the *accomplishment of natural growth*. In this parenting style, children's development is understood as unfolding spontaneously, and good parenting requires primarily provision of food, shelter, medical care and other basic support. Given the economic and social challenges faced by many of these parents, these activities required much of the available energy of their parents.[16] While Lareau describes the clear benefits of such a model of parenting (less sibling conflict, children better able to negotiate

---

ways that ignore the complexities of its relationship to race and gender. For efficiency's sake, I follow the lead of the authors I quote in using categories such as working and middle class, at times without the careful contextualizing of racial, gender, geographic, and other elements at play. I recognize that I may in fact provide an apt case study of why talking about class in appropriately contextualized ways is quite difficult to do well.

14. Lareau, *Unequal Childhoods*, 4.

15. Ibid., 238.

16. Ibid., 238–39.

free time and interaction with peers, less pressure and more freedom from assessment in everyday activities), these practices are not afforded respect and value by important social institutions such as schools, social service agencies, and medical institutions. [17] As Lareau noted: "There are signs that middle-class children benefit, in ways that are invisible to them and to their parents from the degree of similarity between the cultural repertoires in the home and those standards adopted by institutions.[18]"

Our program, like schools and other social service institutions, assumed that the model of concerted cultivation was a shared value with the mentors from the home communities of the adolescents with whom we worked. However, we were asking many of the mentors to engage in a form of relationship with young people that was potentially culturally foreign. Asking that adults move into a more peer-like relationship with adolescents and spend a lot of time providing adult direction for an enrichment project was not a normal form of relationship valued in working-class and impoverished communities. Given this possibility, it is not surprising that many of the mentors did not leave the cultural logic of their class culture of origin to embrace the concerted cultivation model. Since we coached the young people to expect adults to move into this role, many became disappointed when they saw their middle class peers receiving a form of adult attention and companionship that they were not receiving.

We did not recognize the ways in which our mentoring model was class-specific in the ways Lareau explores. Lareau notes, "Perhaps there is little understanding of the ways in which the middle-class approach to child rearing intertwines with the dominant ideology of our society, making the idea that a middle-class childhood might not be the optimal approach literally unthinkable."[19] Unfortunately, our funding and program ended before we were able to explore what other models of mentoring more appropriate to the other class groups represented in our young people's communities might have been. Our suspicion is that rather than mentoring in a peer-like way, we should have worked with multiple models of "eldering" and "sponsoring" that might have been more intelligible culturally to the adults with whom we worked. While training did explore these distinctive models, the structured activities suggested to the adult/youth pairings definitely embodied the more mutual, concerted cultivation mode. Although

17. Ibid., 76.
18. Ibid., 237.
19. Ibid., 65.

Lareau found the models across racial groups in her study, as explored in the first part of this chapter would also suggest that a racial/ethnic-based cultural analysis of appropriate mentoring/eldering in various communities would have been important to further improve our work with the adult/adolescent pairings.

An Eldering Story

One of our mentors was a local United Methodist pastor whom I will call Rev. Ezra.[20] Rev. Ezra is pastor of a predominantly African American church that has significant outreach with several group homes for adolescent boys in the state foster care system. Several of these young men participated in our program over the years, often with Rev. Ezra serving as their mentor. One year, two of the young men decided to start a community food bank as their year-long community service project. In the city of Denver, food banks require registration with the city and a fair amount of paperwork. When the two young men began to feel uncertain about whether they could navigate this bureaucracy, they were ready to give up on their project idea. Rev. Ezra did not agree with their assessment of their abilities. Instead, he took them to the city office where they had to fill out the paperwork. However, he did not accompany the young men into the office. Instead, he told them about the kind of resistance they were likely to encounter given that they were two young men of color doing something that would be considered unusual by the workers in the office, he coached them on how to respond, and then he made them go in alone to fill out the paperwork. They were not happy about this situation, feeling uncomfortable and unable to complete the task without Rev. Ezra's presence. However, they were unwilling to disrespect their elder, and thus they reluctantly entered the office and successfully completed the necessary applications all by themselves. When the young men told this story to their fellow adolescent participants at the end of the year, it was clear that they were very proud of their new food bank and all of the people it was helping. They told the story of completing the applications with a humorously mixed sense of disbelief and respect for how their mentor had gotten them to do what they needed to do in this situation, and an invigorated sense of their own power to make a difference in their community.

20. Not his real name.

What is striking about this story is that it violates all of the mutuality and shared authority that the dominant culture model of mentoring would say is important to create in order to enable agency in young people. The young men's opinions about what they wanted to do were not honored; they were told by their elder what they were going to do and how they were going to do it. Because of their respect for him, they fulfilled his expectations and learned something powerful about their own agency in the process. His direct instruction and coaching allowed them to experience success in an unfamiliar and vaguely hostile situation. He eldered them, and they benefitted from his wisdom in ways that were empowering and life-giving.

In the early years, as we listened to the young people tell many stories about how their mentors helped them make their projects successful, we learned that some of the strongly functioning mentors/elders of these youth provided direct instruction and coaching on how to navigate such situations, particularly given the sometimes racist response they received. In other words, mentors were able to "elder" the youth into increased agency and sense of self based on their own experience and wisdom. Our program, however, had not initially recognized this form of adult/youth interaction as a successful strategy for the development of agency or as a way of demonstrating respect and care for young people. Addressing the concrete skills of navigating institutions and eliciting adult support for projects, such as making "cold" phone calls to adults in their faith community or in positions of power in the broader community provided better support for young people who lacked these social skills of entitlement. Not listening to their culturally-informed sense of despair regarding their own agency was an important part of being a guarantor of young people. The mutuality model that we were offering of adult mentoring was not robust enough to account for all of the forms of interaction necessary between adults and youth.

Being the Adult In Boundary-Crossing Settings

Throughout the process of designing, evaluating, and re-designing this program we were intensely aware of the social class and racial diversity of our participants. While we were quite attentive to this reality in a number of ways, we did not readily engage an analysis of our own conception of mentoring and how it might be race- and class-specific. Again, relationships between young people and adults externalize largely unexamined, habitual forms of interaction that seem natural and universal but are often culturally-specific, so it is not surprising that we did not recognize our bias. Particularly since our assumptions were largely validated by the dominant culture wisdom about appropriate mentoring in our professional training, noticing the specific ways in which they did not always serve our young participants and their mentors was difficult at first. While we shared with the volunteer mentors a deep concern for developing the agency and wisdom of the young people engaged in the program, our strategies for bringing about this reality were culturally specific in ways of which we were often unaware.

Looking back, we find it strange that our assumptions about proper relationships between adults and young people embedded in the mentoring model was not more of a topic of self-examination and conversation, particularly given that distinctive modes of relating to youth was a topic of some controversy along racial lines among the adult staff during the residential program. Because many of the published theoretical works in youth mentoring come from a dominant culture perspective, they generally reinforced our Anglo, middle-class oriented instincts about adult/youth relations. We often felt very confident that we were advocating the most positive forms of interactions between adults and youth, when in reality we were advocating culturally appropriate forms that worked well for middle class white persons. Transforming embedded, practice-oriented knowledge, such as how adults should act with youth, can be quite difficult.

At the points at which the white and middle-class bias in adult/adolescent relationships were surfaced and discussed, knowledge of and conversation about the varying cultural codes did defuse some of the intensity of disagreement. However, this conversation did not resolve the issue of what good practice should look like in culturally-mixed adult/youth pairings. While it may be more culturally-aware for a white staff member to assume the culturally-appropriate forms of eldering in an African American or Asian-American community with a young person from those communities, demanding certain kinds of respect and deference with their style of relating also potentially re-inscribes the hierarchical relationship of domination established because of the broader racial context in unhelpful ways. It would potentially and appropriately evoke anti-racist resistance behaviors of all kinds from the adolescent participants. Likewise, for an African American staff member to demand the respect common to his home community with white students can come across as inappropriately directive and generate resistance behaviors among white young people.

To avoid teaching the kind of middle-class institutional navigation skills unavailable to many of the working-class adolescents because of fears of imposing inappropriate cultural norms may also re-inscribe a lack of political power that could in fact be valuable to them. As multicultural education expert Lisa Delpit notes, "If you are not already a participant in the culture of power, being told explicitly the rules of that culture makes acquiring power easier.[21]" But how to do so without being patronizing or culturally colonizing is not automatically apparent. In other words, knowing about these dilemmas does not immediately provide a means for correct practice within them, and they can be particularly heightened by the privileged standpoint of the institutional setting if your ministry or program is located on dominant culture turf.

We did discover a few practices that are critical in establishing adult-youth relationships across racial boundaries. Being sure that cultural background of adult leadership has some correlation to the cultural diversity of youth participants, creating opportunities to listen for cues from young people about the kind of mentoring/eldering they find helpful, and being willing to critique and re-shape fundamental assumptions about adult-youth relationships all helped us to improve the adult/youth mentoring relationship.

The Importance of Representative Adult Leadership

The shared consensus between Anglo, middle-class norms of interaction on a cultural level and the leadership of educational efforts and social programs that serve young people who are not Anglo or not middle-class can present enormous difficulties. An important practice in the education and mentoring of adolescents across boundaries of race and class is to be sure that at least some of the adult leadership comes from nondominant communities.[22] Ongoing relationships with leaders in communities that share the cultural background of your participants are also important. These collegial relationships allow both internal staff and external consultative conversations about the limitations of the educational model for a multiracial community when you become aware that they are present (which is probably only part of the time). As Kathleen Talvacchia notes, "The un-

21. Delpit, *Other People's Children*, 24.

22. Delpit also names this as the most critical step in teaching across racial lines in public education. Ibid., 180.

fortunate logic of oppression revolves around the fact that members of the dominant culture often cannot see the ways in which they discriminate."[23] As a dominant culture person working in a multiracial/multiclass community, careful partnering is a critical element to successfully recognizing and de-centering inappropriate forms of ministry practice.

Listening Carefully in Evaluation

Some of our best information about how to train mentors and staff came from the participants themselves. We began mentor training by listening carefully to how the volunteer mentors described strong mentoring relationships in their own lives. While the use of the same language with different levels of meaning is still a problem (i.e. Wimberly's use of the term mentoring was qualitatively different, even though she uses some of the same language that we did), there is a chance to learn from careful listening through processes of dialogue and evaluation. To continually ask what each of the young people found helpful from their relationship with mentors at the end of each session and in other casual conversations gave us clues as to what adolescents needed from their mentors that felt culturally appropriate in their home context.

Some additional reflection on what a common form of relationship between adults and adolescents in their communities looked like with both youth participants and the volunteer adult mentors would have been helpful. For example, one of the images we used in training mentors the second year came from a Filipina participant the first year. She talked during her written evaluation about how the staff the previous year was fantastic, like her favorite tías (aunts) at home. This was a helpful metaphor for an appropriately hierarchical and yet non-parental relationship within her own cultural heritage. Listening for the metaphors, forms of address, and assumptions about relationships that were culturally appropriate could help us communicate the goals we were hoping for the young people and discern culturally-appropriate modes of adult relationship that could serve them well.

23. Talvacchia, *Critical Minds*, 22.

Radical Openness to Differing Visions/Models of Educational Practice

The one element that is easy to name but incredibly difficult to live into in educational practice is openness to the assessment that one's models of youth education are simply wrong for the context. For instance, it might have been worth asking if the mentoring/community service project combination simply was not the best form of enlivening agency in the young people we served. Perhaps we should have been listening to womanist thinkers such as ethicist Emilie Townes, who might have asked us to start with rituals of radical self-love and deepening cultural rootedness within more homogeneous communities.[24] It could be that the model worked fantastically well for middle-class youth, but not for working- and poverty-class youth. This kind of radical questioning of basic premises can be quite difficult to engage seriously at the moment of practice, but may be critical to offering educational and ministry settings that are meaningful across lines of race and class. As Freire notes in the quote at the beginning of this chapter, when working across boundaries of power, constant re-examination must be a commitment among the educational leadership. What Freire doesn't mention is how painful that re-examination can be when it calls into questions one's own competence as an adult leader.

Mentoring with Humility and Strength

One of the reasons adults enter into mentoring relationships is because they believe they have something of value to offer to the next generation through sharing of experience, advice, and time together. One of the challenging aspects of mentoring across boundaries of difference is the reality that one's experience may not directly relate to the experiences and challenges of the young people one mentors. As adults, we may discover that we never had to struggle to keep our parents' utilities turned on by contributing money even as we are trying to complete an education in high school. We may not have had opportunities dry up or access to resources denied because of our class mannerisms, our lack of social connection, our headscarf, or the color of our skin. We may not share the familial values and communal norms that are deeply important to the young people we work with. Trying to develop and sustain mentoring relationships across boundaries of difference

24. Townes, *In a Blaze of Glory*, 115.

requires more humility than mentoring relationships with adolescents who share one's racial, class, and national background.

Humility and mentoring may seem like odd bedfellows. Accepting the role of mentor requires a certain amount of healthy authority: the idea that you have something to teach that is valuable to the next generation. Without this sense of the strength of their wisdom and experience, mentors don't add much more to the lives of the young people than do their peers. However, this pairing of humility and authority is not culturally normative in white Western culture, which suffers from a history of white supremacy that advocates that white culture is naturally superior to other cultural norms . . . more professional, more efficient, and more responsible. Although most dominant culture folks would not consciously articulate such a position of cultural supremacy, it is often latent in the assumptions and advice that they give as mentors, often masked in the guise of appropriate adult authority.

This latent tendency towards cultural superiority means that dominant culture folks engaging in mentoring and education of adolescents from other cultural groups cannot slide into the easy forms of authority and wisdom that come naturally to them. Constant self-examination and conversation with partners from other cultural groups is necessary to result in relevant and life-giving mentoring. Without such self-examination and partnering, what seems like mentoring can actually come across as cultural invasion, dominance, or simple irrelevance. This means that when adolescents are engaging in resistance behaviors, they have to be welcomed as signs that we need to check ourselves rather than as character flaws or ingratitude in the young people we encounter. Taking the time to recognizing such resistance behaviors and asking what we might have done that contributed to their presence in the relationship is essential to the development of a healthy relationship.

Such constant self-questioning can be exhausting, and we may begin to wonder whether we are doing as much harm as good. We may want adolescents and their families to respond to our good intentions rather than resist our efforts. When we begin to feel this way, it is important to remember that our individual relationships with young people are embedded in a social history of domination and structures of power that good intentions cannot erase. Yet, many gifts of self-understanding and learning can come from listening to the wisdom of the adolescents themselves and the communities they represent. To enter into mentoring relationships across boundaries of difference requires the humility and willingness to be questioned and to be found lacking paired with the confidence that such a relationship can benefit both members.

CHAPTER 7

Dreaming Together

MUCH OF THIS BOOK has explored the power dynamics and relational realities of engaging in youth ministry in multicultural settings. While tricky waters to navigate, attention to these social dynamics and their attendant realities are essential to being able to engage in youth ministry that does not contribute to oppression but instead disrupts it, enhancing the capacity of youth from all backgrounds to live into their vocational dreams. In this chapter, we spend some time talking about other essential qualities and approaches to youth ministry that we find promising in working with youth across boundaries of difference. Many of the practices in this chapter have been explored in depth by other scholars and practitioners of youth ministry, who were important in the design and implementation of our own ministry practices. By building on their ideas and attending to how they function in multicultural settings, we hope that this chapter will help you imagine your own ministry in whatever setting you find yourself.

First, we need to explore the potential settings of multicultural youth ministry. Sometimes our imagination is limited when we think of settings and contexts in which to engage in youth ministry. In a congregational setting, we often limit engagement with youth to that paragon of mainline middle class white congregations—the monocultural youth group. In fact, if you look up "youth ministry" in Wikipedia, the definition starts: "*Youth ministry*, also commonly known as *youth group*."[1] The youth group emerged as a model for work with youth in the beginning of the twentieth century,

1. http://en.wikipedia.org/wiki/Youth_ministry, downloaded 6/23/2013.

as urbanized middle-class youth began to delay their entry into the work force and had increased leisure time and a perceived need to channel their excess energies in a positive direction. Churches began to create young people's societies or clubs to organize their free time and to keep them out of trouble, with a religious overtone to the activities. Over the past century, this model has become so synonymous with youth ministry (often with a paid youth director organizing or directing the activities of the group), that we find it difficult to imagine youth ministry without a youth group.

Many marginalized young people do not have access to transportation, free time, or the cultural norms that make participation in youth group a viable option. The youth group has not been as popular a model for engagement of young people in Roman Catholic or African American church settings, and may not be a familiar model to many families. In many communities, multigenerational gatherings and apprenticing of younger people to older people in specific tasks in the faith community is a much more common form of ministry with youth. In many nondominant cultural groups in the United States, age level segregation is not a desirable choice for the faith community. Additionally, youth groups and their practices have arisen largely out of white Protestant cultural settings, which may create a barrier to persons from other cultural groups who try to join them. In other words, they are often culturally-specific in ways churches don't recognize. The resources required to staff and fund a youth group may not be available to every community. In these situations, designing and living into youth ministry practices across cultural boundaries means moving beyond these familiar forms and opening up other possibilities for engaging in ministry.

Youth ministry may take place in a variety of contexts. When we think of youth ministry more broadly, we may consider after-school enrichment programming or club settings, school days off programming, summer camp settings, religion classes in parochial schools, social service agencies, churches, or mentoring programs. However, meaningful work with adolescents may take place in almost any setting, including settings where religious formation may not be explicit, but spiritual issues are deeply engaged, such as public school literature and art classes. Even family and friendship settings, where intergenerational interaction and mentoring of adolescents occurs, may be an opportunity for informal youth ministry. The particular context is not critical, but the quality of interaction and clear focus and purpose for engagement is essential to effective youth ministry.

This chapter names several key qualities of good youth ministry and then explores five fruitful arenas of engagement for youth ministry with marginalized adolescents: holy listening, engagement with arts, discovery and critical thinking, worship and spirituality, and projects and events. None of these arenas are likely to exist in isolation from the others. For example, the function of holy listening connects deeply with engagement in the arts, where adult companions are called to the practice of attending carefully to the deeper currents and significance of the art generated by young people. The practices of discovery and critical thinking enliven the practice of planning for and participating in worship. So, while we have named these arenas as separate practices for exploration in this chapter, the best kinds of work in youth ministry gather up two or three of these approaches with the key qualities firmly in place, often in one well-placed event.[2]

Key Qualities of Good Youth Ministry

No matter the approach or setting of youth ministry, these qualities are critical for any effort worth its salt in youth ministry. In addition to the ideas we have reflected upon so far: attending to the dynamics of power and privilege, sharing cultural capital, negotiating respect, broadening our understandings of the forms of youth agency, attending to resistance and its relationship to race/class injury, and mentoring and eldering with humility, now we want to look to key qualities and fruitful approaches to the practice of youth ministry in multicultural settings.

Key Qualities

Honesty

Companionship

Affirmation

Challenge

Responsibility

Joy

2. Charles R. Foster develops a helpful model for event-centered educational ministry in his book *Educating Congregations.*

Vignette—by Sara Sutterfield Winn

Teenagers seem to know instinctively know when they're being fed a line, or being asked to relate to something that they find irrelevant to their experience. I felt regularly challenged to find material that would inspire them to see poetry as an art form that was fresh, relevant and viable for them as young people from diverse backgrounds.

Integrity, respect and authenticity are buzzwords for youth, as they become more aware of the potential for navigating the world on their own intuition and their own experience. I wanted my students to write out of that place of authenticity in themselves, out of the reality of their experience and who they were at that moment in time.

This hit home for me specifically in one of my literary arts classes, as we listened to a series of recorded poems performed by various artists. They listened patiently to Robert Frost read his achingly beautiful poem "Nothing Gold Can Stay," and they all put on their best student faces when I played Gwendolyn Brooks' "We Real Cool" (they graciously assented at least that they liked the rhythm of Brooks' reading). But their faces lit up when I played Regie Gibson's "it's a teenage thang," which depicts in dizzyingly fast and thumping language the breathless joy associated with sneaking out at night to go dancing, an admittedly edgy topic. After the end of the piece, they looked knowingly at each other. In fact, they looked validated. I asked them whether they liked the poem (all said they did), and specifically what they did or did not like about it. Without hesitation, they all agreed that Gibson's poem was honest. One student, Jordan, used the word "real" specifically. They all agreed that it had put words to the very essence of being that age. They knew that no one was encouraging them to sneak out to go dancing, but that the poem was speaking the deep truth of what it is to be young and testing boundaries, seizing joy and freedom. No other poem we listened to elicited such an enthusiastic response.

Honesty may seem like an obvious quality for any kind of ministry. None of us wants to be deceitful or fraudulent in our daily interactions with the people we encounter. However, in youth ministry of all kinds, and particularly with young persons who are culturally different from us, the temptation to be dishonest crops up more regularly than we might initially realize. Sometimes, we want as mentors to have answers or sage advice for the sticky and complicated situations in which young people find themselves. Born from our compassion and desire to be of use, we find ourselves confidently giving out wisdom that we know is only partial and may not apply fully just in order to maintain a façade that we are competent and able to be of service to the young people with whom we work. Or, when asked about our own choices as adolescents about sexual relationships, illegal substance use, or even just following our parents' rules, we find ourselves struggling with how honest to be with young people, for fear of not setting a good example or tarnishing our image as "good Christians." More subtly, we may want to encourage young people by saying that they can achieve anything they set their minds to, in the process ignoring the little voice in our heads that knows that this will not be easy because of the lack of access to educational resources or social networks essential to success in certain fields. We find ourselves negotiating internally about how honest we should be with young people, often because of our own commitments to their success and thriving.

One cross-cultural capacity of adolescents seems to be their ability to see through hypocrisy and prevarication in adults. Young people often have keen antennae for when adults are not being real with them.[3] We actually lose authority and integrity with young people by pretending to understand more than we really do, or by covering up our own struggles with the mysteries and complexities of life in the name of faithful witness. Because of adolescents' collective ability to sniff out inauthenticity, honesty really is the best policy in youth ministry. When a young person asks about something theologically that you struggle with, it is better to share your struggles and the ground you have traced in trying to come to terms with those struggles than to supply a pat, orthodox answer. When a young person seeks advice for their struggles around controversial life issues and choices, sharing your own experience and the triumphs and the consequences of your choices helps a young person trust that you may not have all the answers but at least you are not bearing false witness to them. Finally, when a young person seeks advice about the struggles they are having in their own situation that you have never experienced in your own life, genuine curiosity about their experience and honesty about where you don't share it may be more valuable to a young person than pretending to understand their reality and

3. The title of the Anne E. Streaty Wimberly edited volume on youth ministry points to the importance of honesty with young people in its use of the colloquial phrase "keep it real": *Keep it Real*.

posturing as an expert on how they can navigate forces and realities that you have not experienced.

Honesty does not mean an exhibitionist flaunting of all of your doubts and scandalous stories of your past. Discernment about appropriate vulnerability stands as an appropriate caveat to the honesty is the best policy statement. In the last paragraph, you'll notice that every sentence began with "when a young person asks" or "when a young person seeks." Sharing stories and spouting wisdom when they are not sought by young people in the name of being a good influence in their lives does not serve much of a purpose. Telling stories on yourself for entertainment, support-seeking, or titillation purposes is more about your needs than those of the young people you work with. But when faced with young people's genuine searching and desire to find a way to navigate their world, honesty about what you know and don't know is always better than presenting a false front in the name of pretending orthodoxy, protecting an untarnished image of yourself, or providing a good (but false) witness.

Relational honesty allows for true *companionship*. We talked in an earlier chapter about mentoring, eldering, and other ways of thinking about adults in relationship through a leadership role with young people. The role of companion is a slightly different one. For all of the emphasis on peer interaction in adolescence, this period can feel like a very lonely time of life. As a young person is figuring out the broader world they are moving into and the increased freedom and responsibility that maturing brings, they need good companions of both the intergenerational community and their peer group. Sometimes, young people aren't seeking teachers and mentors, another person to tell them what to do and how, but simple companions. A companion, *com + panis* or "bread-sharer" in the original Latin term, is someone who shares the daily stuff of life with you. Here the adult serves not as guide to the young person, but as the person who is in your corner, the person who is willing walk through the stuff of life with you, and who occasionally may need you as well.

During adolescence, young people experience a dizzying array of changes. Their bodies grow and mature, moving from small and childlike to stronger, larger, and sexually-mature. Socially, their circles widen, and they become more attuned to the networks of status and institutional roles that they must navigate to be successful adult members of a society. Intellectually, their brains gain the capacity to make more complex connections and to analyze what they have taken for granted in new and powerful ways. This emerging strength comes with liabilities in the face of adults who fear they may use this emerging power in ways that could harm themselves or others, creating a fraught situation and increasing conflicts with adults responsible for them in various contexts. Their parents or caretakers shift from powerful, all-knowing beings to fallible humans, creating more responsibility for the young person to figure out their own way and not just fit themselves into the contours created in their home environment. In the midst of all of these transitions, young people often begin to question themselves, their capacity to function, their giftedness and worthiness, and companions provide a steady presence throughout these years of change.

Affirmation becomes a central quality of youth ministry because of these transitions. Young people need others to declare worthy their unique life in its current form, with all of its hardships and joys. Through word and actions, young people need others to express to them that their particular life matters in some ultimate sense. They need to hear that the perspectives they bring are needed, that the experiences they have are worth relating. Affirmation is particularly important for persons who are discovering in new and deeper ways that who they are and where they come from may not be valued by mainstream culture because of racism, nationalism, classism, or heterosexism. For marginalized youth, individualized affirmation may not be enough in these situations. Critique of the norms that automatically declare deficient what should be understood as merely different may be necessary as part of affirmation. Celebration of histories and cultural values held by their communities may also be necessary in addition to affirmation of their individual uniqueness. The cultural work of affirmation that has been a part of the "pride" movements of many marginalized persons must be re-introduced to each generation of young people, who are often introduced to cultural denigration in dominant institutional settings but not to these recovered histories of accomplishment and significance.

For adolescents who have had traumatic events occur to them or who have made costly mistakes already, affirmation is even more critical. They need the mature perspective that helps them understand that bad experiences early in life do not necessarily determine an entire life. We often want to warn young people off of life-altering choices (drunk-driving, drug abuse, felonies, etc.) by indicating that early mistakes can ruin a lifetime. However, young people need to hear that even if bad things have happened to them, their story is not over yet. The life they lived is the one that God redeems. They don't need to be someone else. The experiences they have had are what have made them who they are. They can be critiqued, resisted, celebrated, and transformed in the future, but they are precious because they have happened to a person who is worthy of love, both divine and human.

Related to affirming young people and their gifts and capacities is offering them *challenge.* So often popular culture dismisses young people as frivolous, hormonal slackers and troublemakers. For young people from impoverished families or from nondominant racial groups or national background, this cultural dismissal is often compounded by denigrating racist and classist messages. In such a context, persons who truly take their emerging intellect and other capacities seriously offer adolescents a gift in helping them to not only rise to expectations, but also to begin to recognize their own strength and power. Whether that challenge comes from setting young people to work on troubling community problems, or inviting them to work hard at mastering difficult music for a public worship service, or engaging in complex analysis of data to help a community discern its financial status, trusting that young minds and bodies have the tools to do important and difficult tasks helps young people begin to trust their own strength.

Challenge for its own sake, say excelling in a sport, can help a young person feel a sense of personal accomplishment. However, this sense of competency is multiplied for young people when the challenge is paired with *responsibility.*[4] In a context where adolescents are rarely given responsibility to lead even their own activities, much less to take real responsibility for shared communal events, inviting teens to take responsibility for significant communal tasks that, if they do not do them, will not get done, makes a crucial difference. Developmental psychologist Erik Erikson's crisis for the elementary aged years is often labeled in shorthand "industry vs. inferiority," with the virtue emerging throughout these years identified as competency.[5] Elementary aged children work hard to gain recognizable adult skills such as literacy and numeracy, as well as learning adult roles and the tasks associated with them. While Erikson noted that the classic adolescent task and virtue is a sense of identity, the need to be able to demonstrate competency does not disappear in adolescence. Having the capacity to become truly competent in a task valued by your culture or by the

---

4. David F. White has a helpful discussion of the importance of responsibility in nurturing purposeful living in young people in chapter 6 of *Dreamcare.*

5. Erikson, *Identity,* 122–28.

adults in your community and to engage that task and to be counted on to do it proficiently means that you can contribute. Because so much of what adolescents engage includes abstracted preparation for the future in artificial environments such as school and sports leagues, these opportunities for challenging responsibility are critical for churches and other programs to provide.

The catch for these communities is that offering opportunities for challenge and responsibility also requires allowing failure if the young person doesn't come through. We often undercut moments of responsibility by only giving young people tasks that are expendable or luxury extras or by creating redundancies in the system so that even if they do not step up, the task will still be completed. Allowing the possibility of failure, and even public failure on important tasks, means that adults working with adolescents have to deal with difficult feelings of shame, anger, grief, and alienation. But, without the potential for these moments, there is no real sense of responsibility.

We have slightly skewed understandings of work and play in our culture. Play is all pleasure, entertainment, and frivolity. Work is the boring stuff that adults have to do. Another way to think of work is as the privilege adults have to shape the institutions and communities that affect everyone else, and invite young people into being a part of that. As one of the wiser advocates of youth agency in our culture, David White notes:

> Young people yearn to "do something" and so are expressing a holy desire to meaningfully engage in the reconciliation of the world and their true selves—beyond the frivolous social and recreational activities we provide in hopes of retaining their interest. They yearn to be actors in history and not merely acted upon. Youth sense that the world is full of wounds for which they have resources.[6]

Creating the time and trust for young people to accept challenges and take responsibility for others as they fulfill them allows trustworthy persons to emerge when trust is placed in them.

Often our perceptions of adolescents are that they just want to have fun and to be entertained, to live life with electronic devices permanently attached to their hands, rather than that they desire challenge and responsibility. This brings me to my final quality of work with young people. That is, they tend to resonate with activities completed in a tone of *joy and*

6. White, *Practicing Discernment*, 187.

liveliness. I have purposely avoided the terms "fun" and "entertainment" because these terms are associated more with distraction and amusement than with challenge and responsibility. But adolescents often can discern how to bring a sense of vitality and energizing connection to even the most mundane of responsibilities if they feel they are making an important contribution through their work. I would much rather sort clothes for a shelter, clear trails of rocks, or wash spinach in a gleaning project with a group of adolescents because they are bound to find the joy in it. This is one of the real charisms of youth. Often this sense of liveliness gets mistaken for frivolity, but this charism doesn't require a constant stream of compulsory fun but rather is more about the spirit in which the activity is engaged.

Fruitful Approaches

Holy Listening

Engaging the Arts

Discovery/Making Connections

Worship and Spirituality

Events and Projects

Holy Listening

As discussed in the affirmation section above, nothing validates the experience of a young person more than that of being seen, heard, and appreciated as one currently is. Thus, we have called our first approach to youth ministry "holy listening." Although listening seems like an obvious task unworthy of naming as an approach to youth ministry, fully attending to a young person is remarkably easy to overlook if you are in a setting where you are not simply in relationship with a young person but also have to fund, develop, execute, and staff a program, or if you also have a job, home maintenance tasks, and aging parents to care for. We have borrowed the term "holy listening" from the practices of the Youth Theological Initiative at Emory University, but although this practice may actually include sitting and listening to the talk of a young person, we are also using "listening" as a metaphor. Sometimes no words are exchanged, and the "listening" actually refers to attending carefully to the movements, behaviors, and body language of young people.

Holy listening is a generous spiritual practice of hospitality for the listener. Careful attention can be difficult because there is often lots of air traffic with adolescents, or conversely, almost none. Listening beyond the surface conditions of conversation for the deeper currents, the stirrings of the soul, the existential quests, the sorrows behind the complaints, the deep joys behind the "squees," and the unnamed fears that loom large requires a fair amount of patience and work. This kind of listening requires the time and space to bring questions, dreams, concerns, rants both major and minor. The listener creates this space by providing a non-judgmental but invested presence. In her book on young adult faith, Sharon Parks calls this kind of space "hearth space," the holding place as if in front of a warm fireplace for a young person to pull up a chair and talk heart-to-heart without much agenda.[7]

This careful practice of generous attention has many different functions in youth ministry. In the first place, attending carefully to young people honors the sacred importance of their life, with all of its twists and turns, joys and sorrows. Given the largely age-segregated patterns of life in the United States, teenagers rarely have interactions with an adult with little agenda. The purpose of holy listening is not instruction, not control or correction, not shared distraction, but just committing the time to listen with care to a young person.

Vignette—by Katie Robb

One summer I co-lead a Covenant Group with the Literary Arts teacher. While there was little at-the-surface cultural diversity in the group, we were confronted with difference in the presence of Anna, a white Episcopalian young woman with South African roots and cerebral palsy. Anna was a bright and compassionate young woman, but she had minimal control of her muscles, which made her speech difficult to understand. When she was excited, Anna's limbs would spasm and jerk, so often the most important points she wanted to make were the most difficult to understand.

7. See discussion of the practice of "hearth" in Parks, *Big Questions, Worthy Dreams*, 198.

I had previously met Anna, so I knew that she was very patient with people repeating her words back to make sure they were understanding her right. The other youth, however, didn't know how to listen or react to Anna. It was evident after a few days of "uh-huhs," fake smiles and nods, that they didn't understand her, but wanted to treat her as a normal person. The other teacher and I would try to model the paraphrasing, but the youth weren't picking up on it, or were too nervous to try. Finally one day after class, I sat with the four in our group to check in about their reactions to Anna. We talked about how to paraphrase her or ask her if they were understanding right.

It was like a light bulb went off! We had all kinds of fun both hearing Anna and in the sometimes crazy things we thought we heard, like a game of telephone. Our listening skills all sharpened, not just for Anna's voice but for each individual. The group became very close over the next few weeks, able to express some very difficult personal issues and admire each other at a deeper level of identity. It was truly a time of holy listening.

While the intention of such listening is not therapy, the experience may be therapeutic for the young person. Listening (and by extension asking someone to compose a narrative) often provokes self-understanding in the person generating the narrative for someone else's understanding. Sometimes, in being asked to articulate what's going on for another person, a person comes to understand it themselves and to find out what they themselves think. This learning may be especially important with regards to faith. In the work of Christian Smith and Melinda Denton for the National Study of Youth and Religion, the researchers realized that their interviews were the first time that someone had asked the young people to articulate their personal beliefs about God and faith.[8] While I am not as keen on the value of drilling information and being able to articulate doctrinal claims as they are, I do believe that when a narrative is evoked by another person, in the articulation sometimes we find out what we think, understand, and believe.[9]

8. One of Christian Smith and Melinda Denton's recommendations to faith communities and parents encouraged increased work on "articulation": "We were astounded by the realization that for very many teens we interviewed, it seemed as if our interview was the first time any adult had ever asked them what they believed" (*Soul Searching*, 267).

9. Psychologist Dan McAdams has done interesting work on the importance of

Additionally, if the adults around them evoke and listen to their inner voices and experiences, in time adolescents may learn to listen to them as well, practicing intentionality about their choices and the impact they have on their own soul and wellbeing. Noticing the choices they can make in the face of the circumstances that are placed before them in their life is part of mature thinking about composing a life. Rather than reacting thoughtlessly to the forces impinging on their lives, learning to listen to themselves and the still small voice inside and attend to that voice is essential for young people. Sometimes they learn to listen to themselves because other people listen to them and take them seriously.

This adult noticing may also be the first step in nurturing the voice of vocation. The Fund for Theological Education (FTE), in their work on how young people develop the capacity to respond to a call to ministry, talks about the work of their communities of call as "notice, name, and nurture."[10] A community notices the gifts of a young person through practices of attention, then publically names those gifts and begins to nurture them. While the FTE is particularly interested in young people's call to ordained ministry in the local church, the process is similar in vocational development for all young people. In order to notice the gifts that a young person has to offer to a community, practices of holy listening are essential.

What does holy listening look like? Civil rights era historian Vincent Harding, who worked with youth in his Ambassadors of Hope program, talks about being sure that elders are "keeping a hand on the shoulder of young people," simply staying in touch with them to know what's going on in the midst of confusing times. In our program, especially with kids who were struggling, we'd have adults whose job it was simply to check in with a small group of kids each day. Daryl, in charge of our music exploratory group, had a natural way of doing this. For example, one of the participants "Ben" was Daryl's charge in the residential environment. In an effort to touch base with him each night, Daryl would say, "Ben, are you pulsing?" Meaning, "Ben, do you have a pulse? Are you alive? Are you fully alive?" This characteristically groovy way of asking was natural to Daryl

---

narrative to the construction of self, and the process of creating a life story as a process of developing identity and personality. An interview with an adult gives adolescents the opportunity. See McAdams, "Personality, Modernity, and the Storied Self," 295–321.

10. The Fund for Theological Education has named these three practices "notice, name, and nurture" as central to the VocationCARE practices essential for helping young persons discern a call to ministry. For more on their VocationCARE resources, see http://www.fteleaders.org/preview/pages/vocationcare-practices/.

and a great way to touch base that wasn't intrusive. He just let Ben know he was checking in. Even after the three weeks ended, Daryl would check Ben's pulse now and again through other means of communication, always using his characteristic catch phrase.

Holy listening can be formal or informal. In one sense, this practice is a low-cost, simple approach to youth ministry. It simply requires time, attention, and a safe semi-public space.[11] On the other hand, attention takes some intentionality, because often we are in a mode of parenting, teaching, mentoring, and we fail to take our role as listener seriously. Often holy listening occurs incidentally through the process of sharing art work, when we attend at a deeper, soulful level to what is being shared and not shared. It may occur through conversation while we are engaged in mundane tasks such as setting up for a meal. When young people put themselves out there, whether in words (traditional listening) or through sharing their efforts (art pieces, service projects, worship services), being recognized, seen, noticed, heard, all are metaphors for basic affirmation of the worthiness of their efforts and at a more fundamental level, of them.

More formal means of holy listening might include any number of interviewing practices, one of the great underused tools of youth ministry. At FaithTrek, we utilized Appreciative Inquiry-style interviewing to help young people reflect on their own strengths, places of joy, and places of connection in conversation with one another. Interview doesn't have to mean the adult asks the question and the adolescent responds to it in classic social science research style. There are many ways to pose questions that young people respond to. Whether this involves activities where adolescents to engage in digital storytelling about their experiences, opportunities to create artistic representations of commitments or values that they hold, or a river of life exercise such as the one proposed by Joyce Ann Mercer, structured reflection opportunities provide opportunities for adolescents to experience holy listening.[12]

In order to create the space for conversations to occur that allow for holy listening, often the Third Thing serves well. Psychologist William Pollack explored the usefulness of engaging in action-oriented activities when talking with boys, but the practice is helpful for easing conversation with

---

11. Whenever we are in conversation with young people one-on-one, good practice demands being in a location where we are easily observed but not easily overheard, whether in an office with a window, on a park bench, or in an ice cream store or other busy public place.

12. See Mercer, *GirlTalk/GodTalk*, 135.

all kinds of young people.[13] The Third Thing allows both adult and youth to officially be focused on something else, but provides the opportunity for careful talking and listening to occur. Whether this is driving a car for parents, making cookies, washing dishes, shooting hoops, folding paper cranes for an art installation, shelling peanuts, playing cards, or painting over graffiti in the neighborhood, the opportunity to talk often comes through moments of repetitive work or entertainment activities that don't require much cognitive attention, leaving room for casual conversation to erupt. Some adult mentors use this practice quite intentionally, being sure that they find opportunities to chat with all of the young people in their group through a series of such Third Thing activities. We often had mentors who would set up a chess board in the lobby and wait to see who would drop in for a game, or who would bring a huge sack of peanuts in their shells to a public space and sit down and start shelling, snacking, and talking (peanut allergies might cause a different choice). The Third Thing can be any number of particular activities, but generally provides the opportunity for informal holy listening to occur by taking the center of attention and shifting the intense focus of face-to-face conversation to allow side conversations to occur.

A variation of the Third Thing technique my involve simply providing items in the middle of a table—such as pipe cleaners, paper with markers, pens, and Play Doh—when difficult conversations need to happen in a community. These objects can also provide a Third Thing that can help get young people through intense relational work. Particularly in conflict settings, the ability to be paying attention to something other than each other can be particularly helpful. While we want the person's full attention, sometimes this is too hard for adolescents whose selves are not grounded and secure in their adult identity, and a physical outlet for the anxiety of such a conversation helps the conversation along. These tools also allow for dreaming about "what might be" while conversing about other anxiety-provoking topics, such as ideas for future paths or relationships or communities that young people hope to be a part of.

Engaging with Arts

Sitting around a table dreaming dreams about what can be possible provides a helpful transition into a conversation about engaging with arts. Art

13. Pollack, *Real Boys*, 101.

forms create a venue for dreaming a future of new possibilities, for cultivating imagination for the world as it could be, as well as for expressing
the struggles and beauty of what is. The late American poet Audre Lorde
wrote an essay in which she connects the relationship between vocational
discernment and the act of creating:

> [I]t is through poetry that we give name to those ideas which are—
> until the poem—nameless and formless. . . . If what we need to
> dream, to move our spirits most deeply and directly toward and
> through promise, is discounted as a luxury, then we give up the
> core—the fountain—of our power . . . we give up the future of
> our worlds.[14]

Lorde describes how art provides an opportunity for self-discovery
by giving form to the deepest desires and patterns of our spirits. Just as
responding to interview questions often allows youth to formulate ideas
that previously were only latent, sometimes the written word, the painting,
the song teaches the artist what they already know by externalizing it and
allowing them to engage it. Various art forms, including those that don't
involve words, can be a place of self-exploration, of discernment, of figuring out how youth feel and understand the world, God, and their sense of
belonging within all that is.

Arts have historically been a legitimate space of voice and impact
for marginalized persons, particularly during historical periods where they
have had limited access to the power structures or official channels of communication in a society. While one aspect of youth ministry with marginalized adolescents involves helping them to develop the social and cultural
capital to be a presence in the institutional structures that impact their
lives, art forms may be a place to develop this voice and agency that feels
safer to young people from nondominant communities. Whether they experience a sense of alienation because they are adolescents or because they
are from marginalized communities, young persons may discover that, as
educator Maxine Greene describes, "one way of finding out what they are
seeing, feeling, and imagining is to transmute it into some kind of content
and to give that content form."[15] She goes on to describe how participation
in creating art generates a space of freedom through the process of being
"an initiator and an agent," choosing for themselves amongst enlarging

14. Lorde, *Sister Outsider*, 24.
15. Greene, *Releasing the Imagination*, 137.

possibilities.[16] Greene also speaks to the need for teachers and other adults who work with young people to imagine their way out of cultural assumptions that arts are only for privileged persons with access to certain kinds of resources. She notes, "It demands imaginative action many times for teachers to realize that youngsters who see different (who have been reared in poverty or come from distant places) have something to say about the way things might be if they were otherwise."[17] Trusting the capacity of young people to engage in serious expression and analysis through artistic forms invites them into the practice of imagining the world and speaking about their visions to a wider public. These skills are essential stepping stones and nascent expressions of vocation in the world.

The arts have historically served as a means for sacred expression and prayerful reflection. Whether through painting, poetry, or music, almost any art form has been utilized to express deep connection to God, creation, and the stories of the tradition. Apprenticing into art forms common to the religious community has been a form of youth ministry for centuries, as apprentices learned to sculpt in cathedrals, write in calligraphy, sing the folk hymns and ballads of the faith community and accompany them with whatever instruments were available, even if it was only one's voice in the fields.

Art also connects us to God and to people around us through the vulnerability of offering ourselves and our creations to one another. A creative writing teacher at the Denver School of the Arts, Azar Kohzadi, begins her interpretation to parents of her middle school creative writing class by naming the human significance of being a writer. Although many people think of creative writing classes as teaching the mechanics of writing and appreciation of great literature, Kohzadi names her actual role as helping young people to see the world more deeply and to share that vision with other people so they can see it, too. Whether this involves creating visions of how the world can be different, or expressing the pain of the limits of current reality, or expressing the sources of joy one finds in life, arts create genuine connection in their expression and sharing, a key part of spirituality. These opportunities for either individual or collaborative artistic work invite young people to make a true contribution to other people through sharing their visions of beauty and sorrow. As educator Maxine Greene puts it: "They are challenged to become active learners, not simply passive receivers of predigested information. They are asked, with increasing

16. Ibid., 22.
17. Ibid., 34.

frequency, to tell their stories, to pose their own questions, to be present—from their own perspectives—to the common world."[18]

At FaithTrek one of the things we discovered about engaging arts with marginalized youth is that often they had talents that the adults around them didn't have. The youth could become experts and leaders on projects and pieces with very little help from adults because of their gifts. To invite youth to engage these passions in their vocational searching allowed them to speak in a language in which they were often more expert than the ones they were called upon to use in school or in other environments.

Starting an arts program does not have to be terribly expensive or intimidating. In your community of faith or broader community, look around to see if there are artists hidden in your midst who can mentor young people as adults just a little further down the road.[19] Many communities of faith already have instruments such as pianos or organs available, as well as adequate space for drama troupes, dance troupes, and choirs to rehearse. During our years at FaithTrek we engaged adolescents with spoken word, drama, creative fiction writing, poetry, visual arts, and found art. Other groups such as Spyhop have engaged young people with digital storytelling and filmmaking, much easier now that even basic technology available for check out from public libraries allows for capturing and editing images. Other important programs such as Moving in the Spirit in Atlanta have engaged dance with marginalized young people, creating powerful youth-driven choreography that expressed the struggles of their daily lives and their dreams for a better world.[20] Even writing sermons and creating short films or dramas for worship engages youth in artistic expressions of their beliefs and invites them to put themselves out there to say something significant in a public space.

18. Ibid., 34.

19. Ito et al. explore how relationships between adults and adolescents in a digital interest-driven environments are distinctive from a conventionally authoritative role: "Unlike instructors in formal educational settings, however, these adults participate not as educators but as passionate hobbyists and creators, and youth see them as experienced peers, not as people who have authority over them." Having a more experienced someone who influences the learning environment without direct instruction is an increasingly common way of holding authority in collaborative digital environments, and would be a useful model to consider for mentors in arts-based engagement in youth ministry. See Ito et al., *Living and Learning*, 82.

20. For more information about these fine organizations doing significant work with young people, see www.spyhop.org and www.movinginthespirit.org.

If you don't have artists in your faith community or among your available mentors, often artist guilds feel strongly about young people having access to engage the artistic forms they are passionate about, and thus they engage in community service and outreach projects. Asking them to visit occasionally to get your group started and later to critique and improve once pieces are created is a great way to enhance the day to day accompaniment of nonexpert mentors. Starting small, low-budget, and with local support means that programs are more likely to be sustainable in the long run. Creativity thrives within boundaries, and sometimes having limits to what is available in terms of materials, leadership and space can force ingenuity and novelty in exciting ways.

Worship and Spirituality

As I mentioned in the previous section, worship practices are a great place to engage the arts with youth, and spiritual practices have long been linked with the arts. As with engagement with the arts, participation in worship and spiritual practices can cultivate faithful imagination in a presumed world of significance and power. Worship and prayer both offer connection with divine power and often with the experiences of other faithful generations who have struggled and thrived. While we often think of traditional worship as static or boring to adolescents, religious traditions are treasure troves of humans asking the same existential questions over millennia. Developmental theorist Sharon Parks calls traditions, particularly religious traditions, a "gift to the faithful imagination."[21] By this, she means that the artifacts and stories generated within a religious tradition are the raw materials that young people can incorporate in their own search for meaning and purpose, if they are offered as gifts to inspire young people and not as fences to contain them.

We often underestimate this connection between young people and the prior generations of faithful believers, but when youth are introduced to the humanizing back stories of certain worship practices, hymn texts, prayers or creedal formulas, they can be inspired by them and begin to feel connected to the questions and quests of generations of believers before

21. "Even in a time between stories, if the great traditions offer their images—stories, symbols, and songs—less as dogma and more as gifts to the work of a faithful imagination—then with critical awareness they can be received as finite vessels to be treasured, reshaped, or cast aside according to the relative usefulness" (Parks, *Big Questions*, 276).

them. As educational theorist Kieran Egan notes, adolescents are often attracted to the heroic, by which he means "ready association with transcendent human qualities, or human qualities exercised to transcendent degrees."[22] Often we assume that adolescents only want worship experiences that reflect their own music and cultural preferences. However, adolescents also seek wisdom beyond themselves. They are attracted to practices that seem authentic, exotic, or unusual as much as they are attracted to worship practices that reflect their own experiences. Historic practices of worship can provide opportunities for young people to expand their experiences beyond the tyranny of the here and now, and to draw upon the wisdom and insight of thousands of years of faithful persons. To do so requires practices of discovery and challenging engagement with the tradition, not mere exposure to weekly worship. This engagement can truly broaden the resources of young people in their own struggles to find a place in the world.

Engagement in contemplative prayer practices develops an important capacity for vocational reflection, the capacity to listen through stillness and reflection for the inner voice.[23] Communal prayer practices can also initiate connection to the joyful exuberance of the Spirit at work. Participation in contemplative and communal practice helps young people develop attention to what brings them life and what really matters to them, helping to shift their focus to these things. Communal practices common to communities of faith include song, testimony, proclamation, and shared prayers of the people, as well as sacramental practices such as communion. Individual practices may include journaling, contemplative art practices (with clay, *Lectio Divina*), or historic practices of contemplative prayer. However, many youth report deep connection and focusing occurs for them through more active practices such as running or swimming, where bodily exercise or other repetitive actions have a rhythmic, mind-clearing effect that leads to renewed focus and clarity. The kind of spiritual practice chosen does not matter so much as the attraction the young person has to the practice and the regularity with which they practice it.

What is the best way to introduce a new spiritual practice to young people? Educational theorist Kieran Egan argues that adolescents have an attraction to the exotic or novelty in a topic. For this reason, many youth

---

22. Egan, *The Educated Mind*, 90.

23. Mark Yaconelli has done important work on introducing contemplative practice into youth ministry. See his discussion of inviting young people into such prayer practice in *Contemplative Youth Ministry*, 189–96.

ministers introducing prayer practices often choose forms of prayer or meditation, such as *Lectio Divina* or praying with icons, with which young people are not particularly familiar. While these are ancient practices from the Christian tradition, they seem unusual because of their lack of common use in many Protestant and evangelical Christian settings, or the lack of use with children in many Christian communities. Their novelty generates some interest that may sustain the kind of repetition required for the practices to become meaningful. Other helpful qualities in a prayer or worship practice would include bodily engagement, settings that encourage reflective practice (a special prayer closet or room stocked with candles and cushions and supplies for meditative art), and a leader who is confident and non-apologetic as they introduce the practice.

Another classic approach to generating interest in worship is putting young people into leadership roles. As we know, one of the best ways to learn material is to teach it to another person. Likewise, one of the best ways to help young people appreciate and understand what is going on in communal worship is inviting them to lead it. For example, writing a sermon requires understanding the elements of good preaching and textual interpretation, which helps young people to appreciate the craft of preaching while listening to sermons later. Leading liturgy gives young people an appreciation for what it takes to pray in public well, and an opportunity to listen carefully to the words and images of the prayers they are leading. Responsibility for visual media in worship leads to careful attention to the message of the sermon to choose the right images to embody the ideas being shared. Repetitive practice in choral rehearsal of a song inscribes both tune and text into the soul in a way that it is available later to their meaning-making in daily life. Creation of artistic elements of worship, whether baking bread for communion, writing songs to sing, or creating visual representations in images invites young people to offer themselves and their gifts in ways that are appealing to them.

One way that this approach fails is when communities patronize young people by not honoring standards of practice for youth leadership of worship. While we are perfectly happy to hold young people to high standards of practice when we introduce sports or music, we often fail to offer challenge as they are engaging and leading worship. Seeking excellence in practice communicates to young people that worship and prayer matter enough to try to do them well. Sometimes that excellence in practice requires attention to the history of how things have been done, the structures

of prayers, performance techniques, and about personal spiritual preparation for worship leadership. Learning about how to do worship and spirituality well also requires practices of discovery and making connections.

Discovery and Making Connections

We have been talking about multicultural religious education throughout
the book, and here we want to talk a little bit more directly about education.
Education in communities of faith, particularly Protestant communities of
faith in the United States, often is held with some level of suspicion. As
a young person, I (Katherine) was told to be careful of what I studied in
college, because certain majors would "destroy my faith." We often have
seminary graduates who enter into churches that basically tell them that all
of their book-learning needs to be forgotten because it is useless.

This tension between education, critical thinking and faith makes little sense in Jewish communities where the role of rabbi is as much scholar
and teacher as it is ritual functionary and pastoral caregiver, and the adjec-
tive "learned" is not considered demeaning. Certain strands of Christianity
have been in tension with scientific thinking dating at least back to the
Renaissance, currently marked by tensions which arise in our context in
terms of arguments over teaching evolution or comprehensive sexuality
education in schools.

Because of these suspicions about the relationship of learning to faith,
committing to serious education in communities of faith often proves difficult. However, young people's brains are making more complex neural
connections post-puberty, and new kinds of thinking are available to them.
They are able to begin to compare systemic ways of organizing knowledge
(theories), the kind of formal operations that Piaget noted allowed for the
study of algebra after the age of twelve. To ignore this development in young
people is to put at risk their relationship to the Christian tradition. James
Fowler, when lecturing on his research on faith development, occasionally
told stories about the emergence of the twelve year old atheist. These were
adolescents whose new-found brain development and questioning was not
met with excitement in their communities of faith but rather with calls for
orthodox commitment to the doctrines of the church. Forced to choose between what they were learning in school and their faith commitments, they
decided they couldn't believe anything the church told them. This response

negates the emerging strengths of young people rather than embracing these newly found capacities.

Engaging young people in practices of discovery and making connections honors their emerging capacity for complex thought. At the point where their brains are gaining the capacity to sort through information and connect it into complex schemas of how the world works, young people need contexts where they can explore religious knowledge and put it into conversation with what they are learning about the world in school and in their social circles. This process of meaning-making is one of the basic human capacities and desires. Young people find it helpful to be given the opportunity for relevant, engaged learning in their communities of faith, education that takes their minds seriously as they grow older. Additionally, for young people who do not have access to structures of power and the cultural capital of systemic and critical thinking available in higher education, this commitment to engaging learning becomes even more significant.

We have chosen to talk about discovery and making connections rather than education for a few reasons. First, marginalized adolescents have often not had great experiences in formal institutions of learning such as schools. Because their home cultural context may be quite different than the one that shapes their schools, the expectations and norms of interaction in schooling contexts can be alienating.[24] Many highly intelligent nondominant young people express concern that success in academic settings might betray their capacity to connect culturally with their peers. Additionally, adolescents already spend an enormous amount of time in formal school settings, often the equivalent of a full work week including homework, so they will resist additional school-like activities.

Fortunately, churches and other nonacademic settings have the freedom to engage in discovery and making connections with significantly more freedom than do formal schooling settings. Right now, public school teachers have very little ability to choose curricular resources, learning activities, and outcomes for learning for and with their students because of the increasing standardization of all of these processes in publically-funded settings. By contrast, all of the settings for youth ministry that we have discussed are able to pursue topics relevant to young people's questions and concerns, not just a bank of knowledge considered important and standardized for their future use. For the most part, unless responsible to a granting or other funding source, programs in faith communities don't

---

24. Gonzalez et al., *Funds of Knowledge*.

have external parties demanding measurable outcomes (except sometimes in attendance, which is often counter-productive to this task). They are able to pursue the issues and interests of the young people they serve, and find the means to create a rich educational environment that is challenging and engaging. Informal educational settings with adolescents can reflect all of the wild and wonderful ways that learning happens and invest in them instead of being limited to a classroom setting. Mentors can engage young people in experiential education, immersion experiences in contexts that are unfamiliar to them, participation in rich and vibrant intergenerational settings and groups . . . the possibilities are limitless.

An important starting point for deciding what to pursue educationally is to find the questions and concerns that are what the young people care most about. David White calls these the heart themes of young people, a variation on Freire's idea of generative themes.[25] As White notes, sometimes young people have been taught not to notice or advocate for their own curiosity and desires through an educational system that has already decided which questions and answers will be pursued. This formation means that young people sometimes have to learn how to notice what they care about and how to ask important questions. I have had countless youth ministers say, "I know I'm supposed to study stuff that they care about with them, but when I ask them they don't have any ideas about what they want to learn." White's book offers many helpful suggestions about how to help young people discern the things they care most deeply about. One easy way to begin to find out what matters to your young people is to simply take a walk through their neighborhood or environments where they spend a lot of time and begin to ask questions such as: What does what you see tell you about where there is need? What do you see that breaks your heart? This analysis of their home environment serves as a starting point to discern what questions and issues matter. Also, listening to the struggles that are happening in their high school, or the requests that young people resist, or

---

25. Freire notes, "It is not our role to speak to the people about our own view of the world, nor to attempt to impose that view on them, but rather to dialogue with the people about their view and ours. We must realize that their view of the world, manifested variously in their action, reflects their *situation* in the world" (Freire, *Pedagogy of the Oppressed*, 77). For Freire, careful attention to how people understand the world and their possibility to act upon it is essential to the process of education. David F. White picks up the complex nature of this understanding and emphasizes its affective and commitment dimensions by talking about the importance of the "generative heart themes" of young people in his *Practicing Discernment*, 98.

the things they get angry about can give you a clue as to where their energy for learning lies.

Engaging in discovery with young people around things they care about takes care of one concern that many adults have about teaching young people: their boredom. Another concern is lack of expertise in the things that young people want to learn about. Fortunately, in the age of internet, reliable information about almost anything can be found online. One stance that adults can take is not that of expert, but as helper in finding out which resources are more likely to be reliable and sending them off to find out more about it. In the age of such limitless information (free through public libraries even in remote rural locations), discovery means not only having access to this content, but increasing ability to sift information wisely . . . checking sources for reliability, leveraging the adolescent hypocrisy meter and the sense of rebellion against power to figure out how to find trustworthy sources of knowledge and eliminate spurious ones.

Often, educational programs for adolescents shift from topic to topic week to week as a strategy to alleviate boredom and to increase interest levels in young people. However, this strategy has unexpected costs. Young people like to have exhaustive knowledge about something as a means to control uncertainty and to gain a handle on how much one has to know to become an "expert" on a topic. Often adolescents enjoy gaining extensive expertise on certain (often limited) realms of knowledge, such as the music of one band, or the stats of a certain team, or the fashion line of a particular designer.[26] Educators can leverage this desire for mastery through allowing youth to chase individual interests to become "experts" in particular topics. While there is an important role of dabbling and having broad exposure to find something that matters to young people, extensive dabbling may leave young people feeling dissatisfied that they never get a handle on anything.

Projects/Events

Our final fruitful approach to youth ministry involves youth designing and completing projects and events. The satisfaction of taking on a large project or hosting an event and seeing it to fruition counters a societal image foisted upon particular youth of being in need of care/control/containment. Due

26. "By learning about *something* exhaustively, one gains the security that the world is in principle knowable. So one reduces the threat that one is insignificant or at the mercy of an unknowably vast reality (emphasis original)" (Egan, *Educated Mind*, 87).

to the extended nature of preparation for full participation in our economic structures, adolescents often feel left out in terms of contributing or making a difference. In this holding period of constant preparation for an uncertain future, to be able to take the passions and concerns that they have and turn them into a concrete response now allows them the satisfaction of taking on something and seeing it through.

Although young people don't always appreciate calls to contribute to ongoing institution-building and maintenance, they do often enjoy taking on a time-limited project with a start and a finish that makes a real contribution to the world. In doing so, they participate in long history of faithful young people in service on behalf of faith commitments such as love for neighbor and thirst for justice and peacemaking. For example, high school students played an extensive role in marches and protests during the Civil Rights Era movements for increased freedom for African Americans. These significant, short-term projects may not fix the world, but they can be concrete steps in the long, slow bend toward justice.

An important aspect of taking on projects or events with young people is being careful to avoid make-work or false significance where it is not there. The real trick in engaging young people in projects or events is in connecting their concerns to opportunities to contribute in a world that is often fearful or dismissive of teens. Events and projects can be difficult to engage when young people have burned some bridges with their adult guarantors or not been trustworthy in such ventures in the past.

What counts as an event or project? Basically, any discrete task or gathering that contributes something to the wider community, requires leadership and organization from adolescents, and connects to something that young people are passionate about. We invited all of the young people in FaithTrek to take on a project over the year between our summer residential stays. These projects took on many forms, but they ranged from the publically significant (starting an ongoing food pantry) to personally significant (hosting a fundraising event to provide funds for a charity dealing with child abuse). Through the years, we realized that some young people thrived while working on an individual project that mattered to them, others thrived upon a communal project that involved combining their skills and talents to bring about something truly special. For example, we had several members of an extended family host a festival in their faith community designed to heal a rift among longstanding adult subgroups that had been in conflict. The young people hated that the church had this kind of simmering conflict, and designed an event that allowed various members of the community to have a positive experience together.

For all of these projects, the young people engaged in a period of discernment where they identified something that they cared deeply about. We encouraged them to move beyond the big and obvious issues to the ones where they may have some possible sphere of control or contribution and personal investment. We invited the young people into a period of learning about the issue they cared about and analyzing how it played out in their community. This period of due diligence also involved engaging in connection-making with others who had addressed the issue in the community to see what had been done before and how it turned out. Young people identified existing resources, such as contacting other organizations working on this issue in their community and asking what they need or contacting people in their circles of relationship that already are connected to the issue or concern. The projects and events did not always provide direct service. Sometimes the young people leveraged their artistic gifts in an event to raise awareness about an issue and funding for an organization working to address it. The key to the project was that it combined the values and roles and strengths of youth with an outlet for making a responsible and challenging contribution to the community.

Sending Forth

We began this book with the claim that engagement in youth ministry across lines of difference implies both risk and responsibility for persons of relative social privilege who work with nondominant young people. We end the book ever attentive to the inherent possibility of colonizing practice in multicultural educational encounters, but hopeful that attention to the power dynamics and cultural realities at work in such settings might mitigate the risks and allow for transformative encounters to occur. In such work, we hope that the social and cultural capital available to dominant culture persons might be shared to increase capacity for nondominant young people to live fully into their sense of vocation. Such a reality requires enlivened dreams of God's desires for them in the world and invigorated agency for making those dreams a reality. For the adults involved, multicultural youth ministry also requires constant cultural negotiation, support and transformation of resistance, self-critical attention to one's practice, and willingness for humble conversion. While this kind of youth ministry practice requires special skills and particular commitments, we hope that our exploration of them has encouraged you to commit to nurturing the different dreams of young people from communities other than your own.

Appendix 1

A Typical Day at FaithTrek

7:00–9:00 a.m.	Rise/Shower/Breakfast in Dining Hall
9:00 a.m.	Community Gathering/Announcements
9:30–11:30 a.m.	Exploration Groups (structured class time)*

- Religion & Politics
- Race, Gender, and Class
- Religion and Care for the Earth
- Religion and the Urban Landscape

11:30–12:30 p.m.	Lunch
1:00–3:00 p.m.	Arts**

- Visual arts
- Drama
- Dance
- Literary arts

3:00–5:00 p.m.	Free time
5:00–6:00 p.m.	Dinner
6:30 p.m.	Evening worship/Town Hall***
7:30–8:30 p.m.	Covenant Groups (daily "check-in" groups)

   * In addition to structured class time, Discovery Groups also participated in "contextual learning," where students venture out into the local community to engage with their topic of study in context. For instance, the "Religion and Politics" group visited Focus on the Family, a faith-based advocacy group in Colorado Springs, CO. Likewise, the "Religion and the Urban Landscape" group visited Denver Urban Ministries to learn about their ministries with the homeless.

   ** Often, participants from respective arts groups or covenant groups would provide leadership for specific elements of evening worship.

   *** On some nights, we also had "Town Hall," a time for community governance, when we could discuss any issues of concern or conflict that might have risen.

Appendix 2

What is Appreciative Inquiry?

Appreciative Inquiry is an approach for organizational and personal development that builds upon the best in people and organizations. It is "the study and exploration of what gives life to human systems when they function at their best. . . . In short, Appreciative Inquiry suggests that human organizing and change, at its best, is a relational process of inquiry, grounded in affirmation and appreciation."[1]

Appreciative inquiry relies on "The 4-D Cycle," a process used to generate the potential in persons and organization toward positive change. The 4-D Cycle includes:

1. Discovery: "Appreciate What Is"

2. Dream: "Imagine What Might Be"

3. Design: "Determine What Should Be"

4. Destiny: "Create What Will Be"[2]

Appreciative Inquiry was chosen as a model for crafting conversations around identity, call, and vocation at FaithTrek, because of its positive outlook. When crafting conversations around vocation and call, we deemed it necessary for youth to tap into the places where they feel most alive, where their passions are being used to their fullest, and where they feel most fully connected to the world around them and to the universe, at large.

Thus, we crafted a yearlong "project" to follow the 4-D cycle. During the FaithTrek summer community, we crafted a variety of positive conversations that helped to tap into the spaces and places where the youth could articulate that they felt most alive. This was the "Discovery," piece of the cycle. Given this data, the youth then participated in the "Dreaming" phase, tapping into their imaginative capacities in worship and the arts to dream about what the world around them might look like where their positive attributes use to their fullest. Next, in the "Design" phase, the youth worked with mentors from their home communities to carry out a project at home which would allow them to put their positive skills and attributes into action to meet a particular need in their communities. Finally, the "Destiny" phase commenced as they worked with their mentors at home to bring their projects to fruition. And, as with any good model for personal chance and organizational development, the youth were invited to evaluate their projects, reflecting upon how their projects invited them to use their best gifts, to reflect upon what they learned about themselves and their communities in the process of carrying out their projects, and thinking about next steps for continued change.

Endnotes

1. Diana Whitney and Amanda Trosten-Bloom, *The Power of Appreciative Inquiry: A Practical Guide to Positive Change* (San Francisco: Berrett-Koehler, 2003) 1.

2. Ibid., 6.

Bibliography

Bettie, Julie. *Women without Class: Girls, Race, and Identity*. Berkeley, CA: University of California Press, 2003.

Bourdieu, Pierre. *Distinction: A Social Critique of the Judgment of Taste*. Cambridge, MA: Harvard University Press, 1984.

Brookfield, Stephen. "Adult Cognition as a Dimension of Lifelong Learning." In *Lifelong Learning: Education across the Lifespan*, edited by John Field and Mal Leicester, 89–101. New York: Routledge, 2000.

Buechner, Frederick. *Wishful Thinking: A Seeker's ABC*. San Francisco: HarperSanFrancisco, 1993.

Case, Karin A. "Claiming White Social Location as a Site of Resistance to White Supremacy." In *Disrupting White Supremacy from Within: White People on What We Need to Do*, edited by Jennifer Harvey et al., 63–90. Cleveland: Pilgrim, 2004.

Collins, Patricia Hill. *Black Feminist Thought: Knowledge, Consciousness, and the Politics of Empowerment*. London: Hyman, 1990; Reprint, New York: Routledge, 1991.

Conde-Frazer, Elizabeth et al. *A Many Colored Kingdom: Multicultural Dynamics for Spiritual Formation*. Grand Rapids: Baker Academic, 2004.

Connell, Robert. *Gender and Power: Society, the Person, and Sexual Politics*. Stanford, CA: Stanford University Press, 1987.

Cordova, Joan May. "Historical and Cultural Context." In *Asian Pacific American Youth Ministry: Planning Helps and Programs*, edited by Donald Ng, 23–39. Valley Forge: Judson, 1988.

Dean, Kenda Creasy. *Practicing Passion: Youth and the Quest for a Passionate Church*. Grand Rapids: Eerdmans, 2004.

Delpit, Lisa. *Other People's Children: Cultural Conflict in the Classroom*. 2nd ed. New York: Norton, 2006.

Egan, Kieran. *The Educated Mind: How Cognitive Tools Shape our Understanding*. Chicago: University of Chicago Press, 1997.

Erikson, Erik H. *Identity: Youth and Crisis*. New York: Norton, 1968.

Felder, Trunell D. "Counsel from Wise Others: Forming Wisdom through Male Mentoring." In *In Search of Wisdom: Faith Formation in the Black Church*, edited by Anne E. Streaty Wimberly and Evelyn Parker, 89–107. Nashville: Abingdon, 2002.

Foster, Charles R. *Educating Congregations: The Future of Christian Education*. Nashville: Abingdon, 1994.

Foucault, Michel. *Discipline and Punish: The Birth of the Prison*. 2nd ed. New York: Vintage, 1995.

Fowler, James W. *Becoming Adult, Becoming Christian: Adult Development and Christian Faith*. San Francisco: Jossey-Bass, 2000.

Freire, Paulo. *Pedagogy of the Oppressed*. 20th anniversary ed. New York: Continuum, 1994.

Freire, Paulo, and Myles Horton. *We Make the Road by Walking: Conversations on Education and Social Change*. Philadelphia: Temple, 1990.

Giroux, Henry A. *Living Dangerously: Multiculturalism and the Politics of Difference*. New York: Peter Lang, 1993.

Gonzalez, Norma et al. *Funds of Knowledge: Theorizing Practices in Households, Communities, and Classrooms*. New York: Routledge, 2005.

Greene, Maxine. *Releasing the Imagination: Essays on Education, the Arts, and Social Change*. San Francisco: Jossey-Bass, 2000.

Gutierrez, Gustavo. *We Drink from Our Own Wells: The Spiritual Journey of a People*. Maryknoll, NY: Orbis, 2003.

Harro, Bobbie. "The Cycle of Socialization." In *Readings for Diversity and Social Justice*. edited by Maurianne Adams et al., 15-21. New York: Routledge, 2000.

Hearn, Mark. "Color-blind Racism, Color-blind Theology, and Church Practices." *Religious Education* 104 (2009) 272–88.

Hine, Thomas. *The Rise and Fall of the American Teenager: A New History of the American Adolescent Experience*. New York: HarperCollins, 1999.

Hobgood, Mary Elizabeth. *Dismantling Privilege: An Ethics of Accountability*. Cleveland: Pilgrim, 2000.

hooks, bell. *Teaching to Transgress: Education as the Practice of Freedom*. New York: Routledge, 1994.

Hughes, Langston. *Selected Poems of Langston Hughes*. New York: Random House, 1994.

Ito, Mizuko et al. *Living and Learning with New Media: Summary of Findings from the Digital Youth Project*. Cambridge, MA: MIT Press, 2009.

Johnson, Allan G. *Privilege, Power, and Difference*. 2nd ed. New York: McGraw-Hill, 2006.

Kendall, Frances E. *Understanding White Privilege: Creating Pathways to Authentic Relationships across Race*. New York: Routledge, 2006.

Lareau, Annette. *Unequal Childhoods: Class, Race, and Family Life*. Berkeley, CA: University of California Press, 2003.

Lawrence-Lightfoot, Sara. *Respect: An Exploration*. New York: Basic, 2000.

Leadbeater, Bonnie J., and Niobe Way. *Growing Up Fast: Transitions to Early Adulthood of Inner-City Adolescent Mothers*. Mahwah, NJ: Lawrence Earlbaum Associates, 2003.

Lomawaima, K. T., and Teresa L. McCarty. *To Remain an Indian: Lessons in Democracy from a Century of Native American Education*. New York: Teachers College Press, 2006.

Lorde, Audre. *Sister Outsider: Essays and Speeches*. Trumansburg, NY: Crossing, 1984.

Maslow, Abraham. *Motivation and Personality*. New York: Harper, 1943.

McAdams, Dan P. "Personality, Modernity, and the Storied Self: A Contemporary Framework for Studying Persons." *Psychological Inquiry* 7 (1996) 295–321.

McIntosh, Peggy. "White Privilege and Male Privilege: A Personal Account of Coming to See Correspondences through Work in Women's Studies." In *Race, Class, and*

Gender: An Anthology, edited by Margaret L. Andresen and Patricia Hill Collins, 98–102. Belmont, CA: Wadsworth, 1995.

Mercer, Joyce Ann. *GirlTalk/GodTalk: Why Faith Matters to Teenage Girls—And Their Parents*. San Francisco: Jossey-Bass, 2008.

Myers, William R. *Black and White Styles of Youth Ministry: Two Congregations in America*. Cleveland: Pilgrim, 1991.

Palmer, Parker J. *The Courage to Teach: Exploring the Inner Landscape of a Teacher's Life*. San Francisco: Jossey-Bass, 1998.

———. *Let Your Life Speak: Listening for the Voice of Vocation*. San Francisco: Jossey-Bass, 2000.

Parker, Evelyn L. *Trouble Don't Last Always: Emancipatory Hope Among African American Adolescents*. Cleveland: Pilgrim, 2003.

Parks, Sharon. *Big Questions, Worthy Dreams: Mentoring Emerging Adults in their Search for Meaning, Purpose, and Faith*. San Francisco: Jossey-Bass, 2000.

Piaget, Jean, and Bärbel Inhelder. *The Psychology of the Child*. Translated by Helen Weaver. New York: Basic, 2000.

Pollack, William. *Real Boys: Rescuing Our Sons from the Myths of Boyhood*. New York: Henry Holt, 1998.

Ransby, Barbara. *Ella Baker and the Black Freedom Movement: A Radical Democratic Vision*. Chapel Hill, NC: University of North Carolina, 2003.

Reddie, Anthony G. "Forming Wisdom through Cross-Generational Connectedness." In *In Search of Wisdom: Faith Formation in the Black Church*, edited by Anne E. Streaty Wimberly and Evelyn Parker, 57–73. Nashville: Abingdon, 2002.

Rodriguez, Richard. *Hunger of Memory: The Education of Richard Rodriguez*. New York: Bantam, 2004.

Sample, Tex. *Blue Collar Resistance and the Politics of Jesus*. Nashville: Abingdon, 2006.

Smith, Christian, and Melinda Denton. *Soul Searching: The Religious and Spiritual Lives of American Teenagers*. New York: Oxford University Press, 2005.

Strauss, Anselm, and Juliet Corbin. *Basics of Qualitative Research: Techniques and Procedures for Developing Grounded Theory*. 2nd ed. Thousand Oaks, CA: SAGE, 1998.

Talvacchia, Kathleen T. *Critical Minds and Discerning Hearts: A Spirituality of Multicultural Teaching*. St. Louis: Chalice, 2003.

Tatum, Beverly Daniels. *"Why Are All the Black Kids Sitting Together in the Cafeteria?" and Other Conversation About Race*. New York: Basic, 1997.

Ting-Toomey, Stella, and John G. Oetzel. *Managing Intercultural Conflict Effectively*. Thousand Oaks: SAGE, 2001.

Tinker, George E. *Missionary Conquest: The Gospel and Native American Cultural Genocide*. Minneapolis: Fortress, 1993.

Townes, Emilie. *In a Blaze of Glory: Womanist Spirituality as Social Witness*. Nashville: Abingdon, 1995.

Welch, Sharon D. *A Feminist Ethic of Risk*. Minneapolis: Fortress, 1990.

West, Cornel. *Race Matters*. New York: Random House, 1993.

White, David F. *Dreamcare: A Theology of Youth, Spirit, and Vocation*. Eugene, OR: Cascade, 2013.

———. *Practicing Discernment with Youth: A Transformative Youth Ministry Approach*. Cleveland: Pilgrim, 2005.

Bibliography

Whitney, Diana et al. *The Power of Appreciative Inquiry: A Practical Guide to Positive Change*. San Francisco: Berrett-Koehler, 2003.

Wildman, Stephanie M. *Privilege Revealed: How Invisible Preference Undermines America*. New York: New York University Press, 1996.

Wimberly, Anne E. Streaty, ed. *Keep It Real: Working with Today's Black Youth*. Nashville: Abingdon, 2005.

———. *Soul Stories: African American Christian Education*, 2d ed. Nashville: Abingdon, 2005.

Wimberly, Anne E. Streaty, and Maisha I. Handy. "Conversations on Word and Deed: Forming Wisdom through Female Mentoring," In *In Search of Wisdom: Faith Formation in the Black Church*, edited by Anne E. Streaty Wimberly and Evelyn Parker, 108–22. Nashville: Abingdon, 2002.

Wimberly, Anne E. Streaty, and Evelyn Parker, eds. *In Search of Wisdom: Faith Formation in the Black Church*. Nashville: Abingdon, 2002.

Yaconelli, Mark. *Contemplative Youth Ministry: Practicing the Presence of Jesus*. Grand Rapids: Zondervan, 2006.

Made in the USA
Middletown, DE
18 January 2019